The

NOVA SCOTIA
HOME *for* COLORED
CHILDREN

The

NOVA SCOTIA
HOME *for* COLORED
CHILDREN

The Hurt, the Hope, and the Healing

Wanda Lauren Taylor

NIMBUS
PUBLISHING

Nimbus Publishing Limited
3731 Mackintosh St, Halifax, NS B3K 5A5
(902) 455-4286 nimbus.ca

Printed and bound in Canada

NB1155

Front and back cover photos: Nova Scotia Archives, Bob Brooks fonds, 1989-468
Cover design: Heather Bryan
Interior design: Jenn Embree
Substantive edit: Eva Hoare

Library and Archives Canada Cataloguing in Publication

Taylor, Wanda Lauren, author
The Nova Scotia Home for Colored Children : the hurt, the hope,
and the healing / Wanda Taylor.
        Includes bibliographical references and index.
        Issued in print and electronic formats.
        ISBN 978-1-77108-358-4 (paperback).—ISBN 978-1-77108-359-1 (html)

1. Nova Scotia Home for Colored Children—Juvenile literature. 2. Children,
Black—Abuse of—Nova Scotia—Dartmouth—Juvenile literature. 3. Children,
Black—Institutional care—Nova Scotia—Dartmouth—Juvenile literature. 4.
Children, Black—Education—Nova Scotia—Dartmouth—Juvenile literature.
5. Orphanages—Nova Scotia—Dartmouth—Juvenile literature. I. Title.

HV6626.54.C3T39 2015   j362.76'409716225   C2015-904318-2
                                                      C2015-904319-0

Nimbus Publishing acknowledges the financial support for its publishing activities from the Government of Canada through the Canada Book Fund (CBF)
and the Canada Council for the Arts, and from the Province of Nova Scotia. We
are pleased to work in partnership with the Province of Nova Scotia to develop
and promote our creative industries for the benefit of all Nova Scotians.

This book is dedicated to those who have found the courage
to rise above their circumstances.

Contents

Why I Wrote This Book

"SOME OF THE MALE STAFF would often withhold allowances from the girls unless we gave them a kiss on the lips," read Harriet Johnson's affidavit, recalling her experiences at the Nova Scotia Home for Colored Children. Formed out of a desperate need, the Home, as it was often called, was one of the first in North America to provide for orphaned and neglected Black children at a time when they were not permitted entry into white orphanages. Harriet's affidavit is part of a class action lawsuit, officially settled in July 2014, which laid out, in explicit detail, the abuses suffered by many of the children who called this place home between 1921 and 1989. Whether the former residents experienced various types of abuses first-hand or were witness to them, it was all damaging. And yet for years, outsiders largely ignored the residents of the Home for Colored Children.

As a child protection social worker and former agent for the Provinces of Nova Scotia and Ontario, I was profoundly moved and genuinely interested in the developments surrounding the Home. As a child, I was fully aware of its symbolism and its importance to the Black community: there was no other institution like it in Canada. At the same time, I was also aware that some things were just not right at the Home.

But it was not always tainted by the dark clouds that overshadow it today. Some very compassionate and caring workers dedicated their time to the children who lived there. Certain notable community leaders invested vast resources and energy. Selfless board members championed its cause and fought to establish its legacy.

So, to go against the grain would be to disturb the dust. As a result, no one really wanted to be the first to speak out. But decades after its impressive beginnings, some former residents found the courage to verbalize their pain and demanded to be heard. Today, there is no question that many children in the Home suffered harm over decades. The question we're left with is, how do the adult survivors find the courage to move on?

In 1994 Charles Saunders published *Share and Care: The Story of the Nova Scotia Home for Colored Children*. In it, he captured the initial dream of the Home and shone a spotlight on those trailblazers whose initiative and foresight brought that dream to life. Their admirable work on behalf of the children cannot be underestimated or forgotten. Unfortunately, the actions and poor decisions made by others, coupled with the flawed and discriminatory early twentieth-century system that left the Home to fend for itself, overshadowed the selfless work of those dedicated ones, those who did what they could with what little they had. Even today, there are former residents of the Home who say that being placed there saved their lives. There are some who called it the only home they knew; others say it was a living hell. No matter where the public rests in the debate as to whether or not bad things happened at the Home, its former residents are entitled to recount their individual stories and experiences. Saunders recalls that when he requested interviews with some of the children who lived at the Home, its staff selected four children to speak to him. Saunders remembers these children having generally good things to say about their experiences, but there was really no way to know if the stories were genuine, or if the children had been persuaded to provide such positive feedback.

Upon reflection, Saunders suggests that, had he been fully aware of the extent of those past abuses, he would have never written the book. Understandably he thought he was doing a good thing by trying to bring attention to what was deemed an important legacy. If he had been aware, I am sure his book would look very different from the one that currently exists. Up until former residents came forward publicly, and until the release of this book, *Share and Care* remained the only full, published reference about the Home's history.

The experiences recalled today by former residents ranges from good to horrific. Their stories lend some credibility to claims that favouritism existed among the staff, that special and loving treatment was given to select children while others were horribly neglected. Those who received special treatment may have well chosen to focus only on the good. Despite Saunders's efforts to capture the spirit and intent of the Home's legacy, the largest element missing in his depiction was the dark secret of abuse that lived within the Home's walls for years. However, like many others during that time, Saunders had only heard what were then called rumours. Many people from the community expressed shock and horror as the stories of abuse became public, surfacing in headlines on the front pages of prominent newspapers across the country.

After his book was published, Saunders did encounter one former resident who told the author about the abuses he'd suffered and who said he wanted to write about it. Unfortunately, the two did not continue communications. Saunders later penned a note to the former resident in regard to *Share and Care*, telling him, "I know this is not the book that you would have written."

Despite the fact that former residents publicly poured their hearts out to the media in the early 1990s, some in the Black community still insisted the abuse never happened. The class action suit may play a huge role in current interest in the story, but just as it was back then, there was skepticism among some in the Black community. Even within my own extended family, some of my distant relatives—former residents of the Home—deny ever experiencing or witnessing abuse while living there. I believe their opinions stem from three things: what they regard as abuse may be different from the actual definition of abuse; they may feel embarrassment and shame in disclosing that they were sexually or physically abused; and finally, a few may genuinely have had experiences that did not involve serious abuse.

While some were relieved when the stories were finally coming out, others were resentful of the media coverage and felt many of the former residents' accounts were exaggerated. Some simply could not wrap their heads around such extreme torture and abuse. But whether former residents' experiences are printed on the front page, heard in conversations, or told first-hand, it is difficult not to be compelled by their stories. The level of violent treatment that allegedly happened within the Home would shock and paralyze any right-thinking person, causing them to question just who was in charge. If only one or two former residents had made such claims, it would be easier to dispute their authenticity.

But the reality is that generations of former residents, many of whom don't know each other, have come forward and recounted decades of horrific experiences. Their stories have become impossible to ignore.

Many former residents share consistent memories about the Home. Stories of children used as entertainment by the staff were common. Children made to fight with each other—even with their own friends—as staff sat back and laughed was a common occurrence. The loser of the fight was told to toughen up. If a child refused to fight another, he or she was beaten. Children were left injured, receiving no medical treatment, and instead were simply sent to their room until the wounds healed. Residents also witnessed children beaten so badly they screamed for mercy. Stories of staff members sexually and physically abusing children were prevalent; many residents witnessed it. Some staff members went so far as to force those children to perform sexual acts on each other.

When wary of such appalling events as those that occurred for decades at the Home, it is up to the collective society to examine what occurred, discern what went wrong, and figure out what can be done to ensure it never happens again. That is the goal of this book. It is not an attempt to point fingers, lay blame, or take sides. None of the accused has ever been charged with a crime. In the book, I do not call out perpetrators by name, although residents have been very forthcoming with the identities of their abusers. For the purposes of trying to move forward from the past, I refer to them simply as 'staff'; however, for those who wish to explore further, these alleged perpetrators are clearly identified in court documents and in the affidavits of former residents involved in the class action lawsuit. Naming the perpetrators would serve to contradict the purpose of the book, which is to facilitate healing and inspire courage. This book is an attempt to learn where and how a functioning, civilized society failed its most vulnerable citizens. It is an honest look at the facts to try to determine what can be learned from the mistakes that were made. Most importantly, it is a step towards helping former Nova Scotia Home for Colored Children residents as individuals, and the community, to become whole.

In order to determine how to move forward, it is important to first understand what happened both on a micro level (the Home staff, families, community members) and on a macro level (the government, social workers, systemic factors). The stories in this book do not represent the experiences and views of every former resident, although many did experience similar abuses at the hands of the same perpetrators. These are the personal memories of some very brave former residents who found the courage to share their tragic stories in the hope that they would provide healing for other abuse survivors. Their pain is real. Their stories are real. Their healing continues.

There are also social workers, writers, and others who have exhibited the boldness, compassion, and clarity of mind to contribute their pain, experiences (good and bad), or insights to this book. Throughout the process of writing, my own motives for the book were questioned and my intentions scrutinized. It is normal for people to become defensive or to take issue with the idea of a book like this, but my motivation in this painstaking process has been to provide a venue for many stories to be heard. As a writer and a social worker, a member of a helping profession, I publicly expressed deep concern about how many social workers involved with these children over decades dropped them off at the Home and never practised what we would consider common-sense basics, such as following up with their wards to see how they were doing. Too many former residents said they never saw their social workers again. Sadly, many social workers upheld appearances of maintaining contact, but in reality most had no idea what was going on with their wards at the Home.

As a social worker, I also expressed deep concern about how adults present in these children's lives over generations—insiders as well as outsiders—could allow our most vulnerable to be subjected to such treatment. Too many eyes were closed to what was hiding in plain sight. As a former child protection worker who took an ethical oath to protect children, I could not help but question how so many could do so little. We are all at fault. So that is my stake and my motivation on a professional level.

My motivation on a personal level lies in my relationships with the relatives, cousins, and friends who are former residents of the Home. I know, from working with many families in crisis and with children who have experienced trauma, that the damage can be far-reaching and long-lasting.

Some former residents are thriving, not having experienced the same abuses as other children. Still others struggle with emotional and physical scars that may never go away. This book had to be written. As a society, we need to discover the part *we* played, where *we* went wrong, and what we can do *now* to fix it.

In an attempt to be fair to all sides, efforts were made to obtain input from current and former representatives of the Home, former child protection workers, and the author of *Share and Care*. With the exception of current representatives of the Home, input was forthcoming and given freely. The views of those who agreed to express them are included in the book.

Regrettably, representatives of the central player, the Nova Scotia Home for Colored Children, declined my request to include input from its current representatives. A letter of apology was also requested. The request for such a letter was an opportunity for the Home's representatives to answer some pressing questions, offer an acknowledgement of wrongdoing to former residents, and provide insight into what further steps could help assist former residents in their healing. Instead, they referred me to a story written by Professor David Divine.

Divine was Dalhousie University's James R. Johnston Chair in Black Canadian Studies from 2004 to 2010. The story in question was an excerpt from his recent book about youth raised in care settings. Divine's reflections growing up in the Aberlour Orphanage in Scotland in the 1950s are a collection of poignant insights into his personal experiences. In the excerpt, he states staff there instilled in him the belief that he was loved, that he belonged, and that he was valued, wanted, and respected. In stark contrast, many former residents of the Home claim to have never experienced *any* of these feelings. Divine's excerpt goes on to assert that the sense of security provided by his caregivers helped him weather the trials of life and to thrive. That was not the case for many of the Home's former residents, who were ill equipped for the world when they picked up their broken, damaged lives. It was puzzling the Home saw Divine's experiences as representative of those of its former residents. Divine clearly attributes his successes in life to the strong foundation he received at the orphanage, whereas many former residents of the Home struggle to heal from extreme childhood trauma.

While Divine's excerpt was his story of hope, it was not the response former residents were hoping to receive from the institution at the root of their decades of pain. All they wanted was for the Home to finally acknowledge what happened and provide some positive solutions and encouragement. Representatives indicated that the Home planned to become involved in the restorative inquiry the Nova Scotia government is currently organizing. In the meantime, former residents wait.

Regardless of society's or personal views about this tragedy, for former residents, their word is their truth. Every person who at one time called the institution home is in a unique stage of healing. Some have been on their journey for a long time. Others have yet to begin. Some are too embarrassed to even call themselves former residents. Regardless of where they are, we respect and honour their lives, their experiences, and their resiliency. The stories in this book will be difficult to read, difficult to imagine. All the more important, then, that we respect each individual experience. The optimistic expectation for this book is that others will come to terms with their pain, remove the burden of blame they have placed upon themselves, and take a step forward on their own private, internal journey of self-renewal. The goal is that we as a society will do away with victim-blaming and facilitate, commend, and support the journey of the Home's former residents toward restoration, hope, and healing.

Acknowledgements

WHERE POSSIBLE, I TRAVELLED TO interview former residents of the Nova Scotia Home for Colored Children for the purposes of this book. Otherwise, we spoke at length over the phone. I appreciate each one and want to thank them for the trust they placed in me, sharing their most intimate and hurtful experiences. I am forever changed by their courage. Not all the former residents I interviewed appear in the book, as several changed their minds over the course of the year-long research and writing process. It became evident that some were still not ready to publicly share. Still, I applaud them for their determination to push through and I encourage them on their paths towards healing.

My research involved combing through hundreds of government documents, case notes, files, and reports. It included filing Freedom of Information requests and speaking to the legal team involved in the class action suit. Wagners Law Firm, which led the class action, was extremely helpful in providing the background and context for the class action suit that was filed on behalf of former residents in the spring of 2011, with initially 62 former residents. The firm's tireless efforts resulted in a successful settlement in the summer of 2014.

In early 2014 numerous attempts were also made to speak to the representatives of the Victims of Institutional Childhood Exploitation Society (VOICES) to get their responses to the suit, the apology, and their input about the healing processes of former residents; however, no response was ever received. In fact, several former residents who initially agreed to be interviewed for this book later informed me that they were advised by a representative of VOICES—a group that provided much-needed support for residents, including the facilitation of counselling where needed and a forum to come together and share experiences—not to speak with me. Given all they endured in childhood, their representative's caution and mistrust was certainly understandable. But as the spokespeople for those voiceless former residents, their thoughts and input would have been invaluable. Whatever the reason for discouraging its members from sharing their stories, I wish only the best for all involved, and I fully support each of them in their process of healing and restoration.

I would like to acknowledge the social workers who willingly shared their opinions, experiences, and thoughts for this book. I appreciate that they were able to look at their profession objectively. I am thankful for their perspectives and their input into how we, as a professional community, can move forward.

I extend a special thank you to lawyer Mike Dull with Wagners Halifax law firm. Even though he was incredibly busy with his work and preparation for the class action suit, he always took time to provide the information I needed, send me in the right direction, and connect me with the right people. He was instrumental in providing many of the legal documents I required as part of my research. I am thankful he agreed these stories need to be shared with the world.

A huge thank you goes to those whose contributions of photos and articles helped to shape these stories.

My family puts up with my many endeavours with a smile and a nod of support. They allow me to grill them for information and at the same time they challenge me in positive ways. It was hard for many to discuss or share their thoughts and feelings about the subject matter covered in this book. There are cousins and other relatives of mine who were former residents and whom I would have liked to include here as well. But like many others, they are not ready. I greatly respect that and would like to encourage them to keep pressing forward. I thank my family for their support, for sharing what they felt they could, and for being in my corner. That includes my children, who have listened to my ramblings about this book for the last two years and have put up with my many hours of pounding out words on the computer through the night.

I would also like to acknowledge that there were members of the Home staff and board, mentioned to me by name, who, over the years, made positive impacts on some of the former residents' lives despite all the hell that surrounded them. I don't name them here, but they know who they are. I would like to thank these people for that tiny drop of hope they placed in some children's hearts.

Lastly, I wish to thank the fabulous editors at Nimbus Publishing who put in so much time and effort to help shape this book into a finished product to be proud of. Your work and exceptional talent do not go unnoticed.

Chapter 1

My Path *to the* Home

AT THE TIME OF MY mother's car accident, my siblings and I ranged from two to nineteen years old. Tucked away in a tiny four-room house in East Preston, Nova Scotia, we were not rich. Still, we managed to get by. But as it often does, tragedy struck us without warning and shook up everything we'd taken for granted.

It was the early 1970s, and as many women in our community were, my mother was employed as a domestic. At this time, she was working in the home of Dartmouth's first and former mayor, I. W. Akerley. My older siblings (and later, we younger ones) always ran down to the end of the long driveway to meet her when it was about time for the community bus to come crawling around Riley's turn, a sharp bend on the main road that spiralled downward. My older brother Gerry remembers standing at the edge of the long driveway one evening, waiting for her in the snap of December's bitter cold bite. She stepped off the community bus and it remained, allowing her to pass in front. As she crossed the road towards him, a car sped from the opposite direction, striking her. The impact sent my mother flying in the air. She landed in the ditch. It was later we learned the driver of that car was intoxicated.

My brother watched our mother in pain, lying helpless on the ground, with her eyes back in her head. There was blood everywhere. These images may never leave his mind. He still recalls the red-stained snow. Luckily, our mother survived, but it would be a long, slow road to recovery.

Days turned into weeks; weeks turned into months, as we waited for our mother to be released from hospital. Our older siblings did what they could to look after us younger ones. But with no money coming in, things eventually turned rough. No one really offered help, and eventually someone contacted Child Welfare Services to report that children were living in the house without a parent. A social worker named Pat arrived and gathered up everyone, except my oldest brother, who had already left and was old enough to remain on his own. (Many years later, we still wonder whether that social worker was the same Pat MacDougall who was dismissed from the Shelburne School for Boys in 1975, after being charged with eleven counts of sexual offences against wards there in the 1960s and '70s. He died in jail in 1999, after being convicted in 1993, but would have been working for the Department of Community Services around the time we were taken into care.)

Pat arrived at our house without warning or explanation. We had no time to prepare. My sister (three) and I (one and a half), being the youngest, were placed in a Dartmouth foster home. Our other four siblings—Gerry, Elaine, and the two others (who do not want to be named)—were taken to the Nova Scotia Home for Colored Children. There was a debate among Home staff about Gerry's age. He was close to seventeen. The social worker, Pat, had already left, so staff members made a decision among themselves that my brother would have to leave. They never explained this to Gerry. They just said, "you have to go, you're too old." Children's aid cuts off at sixteen; however, Garnet, one of the interviewees in the book, was at the Home until he was seventeen, and so were others. Gerry could have simply been seen as an extra mouth to feed in the winter under an already strained budget, or there could have been a lack of beds, or confusion about cut-off ages. But without the advantage of speaking to staff involved back then, I don't have clear answers as to the rationale of their decision.

They didn't give my brother the chance to explain anything to his siblings—just enough time for a quick goodbye and then the staff showed him the door. It was the dead of winter, snowy and cold. He had no resources, no support, and no help. He had to make his way back home on foot, unsure what to do next. After witnessing our mother's car accident, my brother should have received some counselling or support. Instead, he was shown the door. No one ever followed up to ensure his needs were being met. It is not clear whether Pat knew that my brother was forced to leave the Home and was now wandering around alone with no money or food. Nobody took notes.

Eventually, a neighbour, Alice Williams, took my brother into her home and treated him like family. He never went back to the Home, and no social worker ever came to see if he was okay. Even making the long trek back and forth across the bridge to Halifax to sit with our mother in the hospital was an enormous challenge for him, both logistically and financially. Having a social worker to help facilitate that, and hospital visits with her for the other siblings, would have made a horrible situation a little easier to bear.

Pat only returned once to the Home to visit my two sisters, ages thirteen and fifteen, and my brother, age eleven, living there. A few weeks after they first arrived, he showed up to drop off a few Christmas gifts. The children in the Home asked my sister if the man was her father. My sister is biracial; her biological father is white. So when the children saw a strange white man bringing a few gifts, they assumed he was her parent. This scenario shows how most of the children living in the Home had no idea who their potential allies were. They lacked a relationship with the people outside who they could have turned to for help. Many of the social workers did not take the time to build a rapport with the children. Their visits were infrequent and their faces were those of strangers. In the field of social work, we understand today how important it is for children to identify with their social worker, establish a relationship with him or her, and make children feel safe to confide in that professional when they are in need of help. But after the one visit, neither my siblings in the Home, nor my sister and I, still in foster care, ever saw Pat again.

Eventually word of our placement got back to my mother, who was still in hospital recovering from a surgery she'd undergone as a result of her injuries. She learned her children were not at home, that they had been scooped up by a social worker and left with strangers. Like others in the community, she had heard rumours about how children were being treated at the Home. She didn't have proof, but she knew the stories. She had heard about the female staff member who used to sexually abuse the boys there in the 1940s and '50s. She had also heard that the children in the Home were underfed. She felt the Home wasn't a place where she wanted her children. Against the advice of the doctors, she left the hospital and returned home. With no social worker to speak of and no resistance from the Home, she, with the help of a few friends in the community, collected her children: the three that were in the Home, and eventually my sister and I who were in foster care. Because of the injuries sustained from her accident, my mother does not have clear recollection of specific timelines, but her best guess is that this occurred about six months after the accident. She was fortunate to have a volunteer to take care of household duties and child care for several months until she could do so again. But what was most upsetting to her was that no social worker ever came to the hospital to tell her what had happened or where her children had been taken. She had to hear it from others in the community.

Today, one of the major responsibilities of social workers when placing children in a foster home, group home, or any other form of care, is to keep solid records and make meticulous case notes. This paper trail not only ensures the social workers remain accountable for their actions and interactions, but it also creates a permanent record of care so children can later come back and gather the missing pieces of their past. Decades ago, this wasn't always the practice. Many children in foster homes all over Nova Scotia suffered the fall-out from the lack of communication, transparency, and coordination on the part of social workers who simply placed them on caregivers' doorsteps.

Even today, because of the lack of good records, case notes, and visits, some, like I, have hit a brick wall trying to connect all the dots. Some have found records to be non-existent, destroyed, or under-documented. I discovered the claims of some former residents rang eerily true when I filed a Freedom of Information request with the Nova Scotia Department of Community Services in the early fall of 2014.

There were so many things I wanted and needed to know. Weeks and weeks passed with no word about my request. Then, finally: a call. They needed more information: dates, middle names. I gave it to them, hopeful it would lead to the information I needed. More delay. In the meantime, I spoke casually with others in the community, trying to glean what I could from their memories.

After a month of waiting for information about my time spent in care, I received that coveted letter in the mail in November. There was no Department of Community Services sticker or label on the envelope, just that unassuming PO Box address in the upper-left-hand corner. Still, right away I knew where it had originated and immediately became excited. But when I clutched the envelope and squeezed it between my fingers, I wondered how all of the information I'd requested—case notes, reports, names, and dates—could fit inside such a small, thin package. I wondered how my missing memories had been reduced to a flimsy, insignificant white envelope. I was soon to find out.

To my dismay, the envelope included one sheet of paper informing me that the department's records related to my care didn't exist. The social worker had not kept adequate case notes. The file was a skeleton at best. Translation: I was an insignificant soul who had been thrown into the child protection system without even a shred of evidence to signify my time there. It was the end of the road for me. All I was left with was the unmistakable and powerful testament to how poorly the system had functioned. Before adequate policies were in place, social work as it related to child welfare and children in care was haphazard at best. The lives that department was charged to protect obviously ranked low on its level of importance; there was little regard for accountability and follow-up.

To this day, there are no permanent records detailing the people my siblings and I were placed with or the services social workers provided us with during our time in care in the early 1970s.

Forty years later, in the spring of 2015, I managed to track down the foster parent who took my sister and me in, but without any help from Community Services records or social worker case notes. She was a young, single Caucasian woman who lived in a trailer park along the stretch of the same highway as the Home. She has since married and had several children. Ironically, my sister and I attended the same church as her when we were in elementary school, but she never revealed herself to us back then. She was unsure how much we knew then and whether it was appropriate to tell us who she was.

Even though I still have questions today that remain unanswered, that foster parent helped me to fill in the gaps of that part of my past. I was pleasantly delighted by her vivid memories of us. She recalled that we were quiet kids who always listened well and never gave her any trouble. We were shy. When we arrived, she was given very little information about us—she was not told of our background, our family, or why we came. But she took us in and cared for us, never knowing what our family had been through. It was the same story for many foster parents back then, who opened their hearts to take in children without ever receiving any help from the social system.

As more stories of alleged abuse at the Home spread across the media in the late 1990s, Nova Scotia's Black community was shaken to its core. Emotions ran high. Some were on the defensive and others were commending residents for their courage. Prior to the media frenzy, my family had never really had any deep discussions about the stories that were coming out about the Home. I think the sentiment among us was the same: it was a shocking and sad time for all involved. But the community's true thoughts, feelings, and expressions ranged from hurt and disbelief to anger and sadness as residents came forward with their stories. My brother and sisters who spent time in the Home remained quiet publically about the events and firm in their desire not to recount their experiences there. But one day, during a phone conversation with my youngest sister, who lived in the foster home with me, and my older, biracial sister, who lived in the Home, some shocking and sad truths emerged. Our older sister told us she had finally written about her experiences of living in the Home. It was the first time she had ever sat down and thought about all the things she had witnessed and lived through. Deadly silent, we listened to her read the words aloud.

I have tried to block out being at the Home. To start with, I have to remember that me and my siblings almost lost our mother to a drunk driver, and how we were so lost not knowing if our mother was going to live or die. Being twelve years old and being snatched out of your house. Taken to a place with a bunch of strangers ("throwaway people"). Being asked if the stranger who brought you there was your father because he was white. The people in the Home seemed to live in their own world, to me. It made my anxieties worse.

Abuse—yes, we were abused. Being snatched out of our home in the first place without an explanation was abuse...the fact that they left my seventeen-year-old brother in our house by himself to die in the cold. He didn't know how to take care of himself yet.

One day he came to the door of the Home. I don't even know how he made it there. It would have been an awful long walk. They turned him away again. We found out much later that a good family looked after him.

As for staff in the Home, there were some awful ones, okay ones, and mysterious ones. The awful ones urged the children to fight and wouldn't break them up. If they had a favourite one, they would cheer them on in the fight. One incident that stands out in my head is my youngest brother and another male resident. They got into a fist fight that was started by staff. The boy she picked to fight my brother was one of her favourites. He was from the same community she was from. We were screaming for her to break them up. She was a big fat staff [member] and she stood there laughing and egging the fight on. She kept saying to her favourite, "Fight! Fight!" Then the boy bit my brother's fingers until my brother's blood was running out of his mouth. The staff broke them up, and she said to her favourite, "If you can't fight 'em, bite 'em." I wanted to look after my little brother. I was so scared for him.

There was a section at the other end of the building that they called the "new part." There was no heat and no other people. They would take myself and another resident to this section with a mysterious staff [member]. She was a white woman. It was a cold dungeon and we had to sleep there alone. The mysterious woman was very scary. She would never say anything. She would just watch and stare at us. It was a form of psychological, mental, and emotional abuse.

I blocked a lot out to survive, and I didn't do that very well. The Home and the system failed us and still continues to fail people to this day.

Even Black people looked at defenceless Black people as nothing. As the throwaway people. It was like they were thinking,

Nobody else cares about them so why should I? I'm making my money and they have to depend on me. Some of these staff [members] were not healthy people! They had their job, food, acknowledgement from the community. So they wanted to kill the weaknesses they saw in themselves: Blackness (bad), defencelessness (bad), poverty (bad). These are all issues that are still alive today. Are we going to fix it?

After hearing our sister pour out her words over the phone, my other sister and I sat in heavy silence for a moment. Neither of us could find words. We could feel the pain in her voice. We didn't experience what she experienced but we knew how damaging the past had been to her. We could understand how the trauma of her treatment in the Home had set the pace for the rest of her life. Many of her struggles as an adult could be traced back to the lack of support and caring she received from the people in the Home who were supposed to be nurturing and loving. Although she was only there for a short time, it was apparent what impact those negative experiences had on her. In addition, she had witnessed other children suffer serious abuse and felt helpless to do anything about it. As an adult, what is even more difficult for her to this day is seeing those same staff members out in the community, as if all has been forgotten.

When the shock of what we had learned began to sink in, I felt sorry for my sister and other siblings who endured the harsh, negative environment at the Home. The effects would be everlasting. We made sure my sister knew we cared, that we understood, and that we were humbled by her ability to share those experiences with us, even though it was so painful to say out loud.

My hope for my brother and sisters and for other former residents of the Nova Scotia Home for Colored Children is that they each come to know that they did not deserve what happened to them, to see what they saw, or to be treated that way. They are victims of a failed and flawed system. I hope they can each make it to a place of healing, forgiveness, and peace.

A little girl peers through a window at the Home.
NS ARCHIVES BOB BROOKS

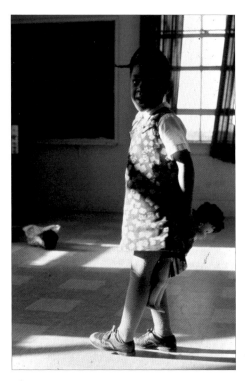

A child holds one of the few toys to be found in the scarcely furnished room.

A child passes an unhappy glare while sitting at the table for his meal.

Children gather around the piano during the broadcast.

Children climb the stairs in the Home.

Two residents fix their eyes on something outside their window at the Home.

Three children play in one of the rooms that a social worker described as bare and scarcely furnished.

Toddlers sit in high chairs lined against the wall for mealtime.

Children return home from William Ross School.

A few boys make their way to the highway at the end of the Home's long driveway.

Children find
abandoned items for
play on a brisk day.
NS ARCHIVES BOB BROOKS

A child licks the
remnants of a
discarded wrapper.

NS ARCHIVES BOB BROOKS

A Home staff member helps a child get dressed.

Garnet shares his life story with the author.

Chapter 2

The History *of the* Nova Scotia Home *for* Colored Children

BEFORE WE BEGIN TO MAKE sense of former residents' stories, we must understand the significance and reputation of the Home: how it served as a symbol of pride, accomplishment, and progression for the Black community, and what the allegations of abuse and neglect mean for its legacy.

According to Saunders's *Share and Care*, the foundation of the Home was borne out of good intentions: to provide a much-needed refuge for Black children who were not welcomed in society and to fill a gap in the services provided for them. Today's social programming is built upon the backs of trailblazers who put in the work to create and deliver vital resources for people in need. The Children's Aid Society itself was created under this very premise.

In 1881 the Society for the Protection of Women and Children was formed in Toronto, Ontario. At this time, the predicament of neglected children was becoming a growing societal concern. In 1873 London, England's, Charity Organization Society (COS), established in 1869, became a model for the United States in the period of economic devastation following the Civil War. Prior to that, in New York City, Charles Loring Brace and a group of like-minded social activists founded the Children's Aid Society. Their efforts in 1853 came at a time when little to no services were available to help poor and homeless children outside of what were called orphan asylums.

In 1891 J. J. Kelso established the first Children's Aid Society in Toronto. This led to what would become the child welfare movement. Kelso was also appointed superintendent of Ontario's neglected children to enforce The Act for the Prevention of Cruelty to and Better Protection of Children, passed in 1893, and was instrumental in helping to establish similar acts across Canada. In Nova Scotia, for example, the first Children's Protection Act was passed in 1906. Originally, the protection of children in Nova Scotia had been delegated to the Society for the Prevention of Cruelty to Animals (SPCA), an organization that had been responsible for neglected children dating back to 1882.

Pockets of agencies, charity workers, and organizers had been moulding and developing this concept of protecting children for decades. But one has to wonder, with the histories of abuses to children in many orphanages, where society went wrong in its attempts to "protect" and "care" for these children. In some cases, a lack of staff education and training placed these institutions at increased risk. In addition, discrimination and marginalization throughout history were so deeply entrenched in policy that prejudicial processes became the common practice. One unfortunate example is what has become known as the "sixties scoop."

In Manitoba, beginning in the 1960s, child welfare workers snatched an estimated twenty thousand Aboriginal children from their families and placed them for adoption with mostly

"Mr. J. J. Kelso, founder of the Children's Aid Society, with W. H. Wightmyer and some of the children."

non-Aboriginal families. The "scoop" carried on well into the 1980s under the noses of authorities who ignored Aboriginal families as they pleaded for this discriminatory practice to come to an end. It wasn't until many years later, following the establishment of the Aboriginal Justice Implementation Commission, that an in-depth inquiry revealed the extent of the discriminatory practices. They shared similarities with the tragedy of Canada's Indian Residential Schools, the last of which closed in 1996. In the commission's 2000 report, advocate Anthony Wood of Gods River told the inquiry, "There was no publicity for years and years about the brutalization of our families and children by the larger Canadian society. Kidnapping was called 'placement in foster homes.' Exporting Aboriginal children to the US was called 'preparing Indian children for the future.' Parents who were heartbroken by the destruction of their families were written off as incompetent people."

In their earlier forms, agencies whose job it was to ensure the best interests of children often became the children's, and their family's, worst nightmare. Countless historical documents depict a culture of intolerance and aversion. Systemic racism resulted in many unfair advantages, often drawing lines between the haves and have-nots. In most cases it left many minorities to fend for themselves in a society that rejected, degraded, and dehumanized them.

The initial vision for the Nova Scotia Home for Colored Children was sparked by James R. Johnston in the late nineteenth century. The first Black lawyer in Nova Scotia and only the third in Canada, Johnston was a prominent leader in the Black Nova Scotian community and as such was acutely aware of the unjust conditions of his time: overt segregation and racism permeated the air; its stench in society was thick and strong. At a time when all other doors were closed to them, mainstream institutions were also closed to abandoned and orphaned Black children, and they were left to wander the streets. Ironically, this was also a time when institutions to house the destitute were cropping up all over the place. Society was recognizing the need to look out for its neglected citizens. Johnston felt there was an urgent need for an institution that would care for and educate deprived Black minors.

As part of a Black History Month event in February 2012, Barry Cahill, a historian and senior archivist with Nova Scotia Archives, presented a paper to the Department of Justice Canada,

Atlantic Regional Office, in Halifax. In it, he chronicled the remarkable steps of Johnston, Dalhousie University's first Black graduate. He described Johnston as a known admirer of Booker T. Washington, and suggested that the two may even have met. Born a slave in Virginia, Washington became a civil rights activist in the late nineteenth and early twentieth centuries. He then went on to found the Tuskegee Normal and Industrial Institute, now known as Tuskegee University, in Tuskegee, Alabama. Cahill said Johnston hoped to create an institution similar to Virginia's Hampton Institute (Hampton University today), where Washington had been educated. This may indeed have been the spark that ignited Johnston's desire to create an establishment to educate young Black people.

In *Share and Care*, Charles Saunders describes the tireless efforts of Johnston and his ally, the Reverend Moses B. Puryear, in bringing to fruition the vision for the Home. Increasing incidences of babies being turned away from orphanages simply because they were Black emphasized the need to press the cause. In the late 1800s, it was segregation or nothing— society's orphaned and abandoned Black children already had nothing, so it was imperative to establish a home for them.

In his book, Saunders recounts an incident involving a Black baby named Arthur MacDougal Scott, whose mother died several days after giving birth at Halifax's Victoria General Hospital. When no one came to claim the infant, the hospital made a plea to the city's orphanages to take him in. They all turned him away; as per policy, none took in Black children. Finally, a Catholic institution agreed to take Arthur in. Sadly, he would be dead before he reached his first birthday in 1913. There is very little information surrounding the exact cause of his death, but this shows how insignificant his short life was truly considered. Unfortunately, such incidents were not uncommon: orphaned Black children were often doomed.

In *The Guardianship of Best Interests: Institutional Care for the Children of the Poor in Halifax, 1850–1960*, published in 2013, author Renée Nicole Lafferty asserts that many local institutions taking in abandoned children during this period exercised segregation by skin colour rather than religion.

> *As much as the city's existing institutions were eager to segregate children for their "best interests," according to their religious origins, so too were many of them eager to segregate according to skin colour. According to Sister Ambrosia of the Home of the Guardian Angel, for example, Black infants were accepted only in exceptional circumstances, "when they are found to be destitute and without any friends to provide for them." Her counterpart at St. Joseph's Orphanage, Sister de Paul, declared that she "prefer[red] not to take such children into the institution, as we have no means of separating them from the others."*

By 1914, and after much advocacy, Johnston and Puryear were finally permitted to present their proposal for a home specifically for Black children to members of the Nova Scotia legislature. This was the first big step in realizing a dream but, according to accounts in Justin Marcus Johnston's book, *James Robinson Johnston: The Life, Death and Legacy of Nova Scotia's First Black Lawyer*, the First World War brought the proposal to a temporary halt. Still, Johnston continued to push his proposal until tragedy struck again in 1915. A few days shy of his thirty-ninth birthday, Johnston was killed in his own home by his brother-in-law.

While the motive for the crime remains unknown, records indicate Johnston's cause of death as a fractured skull and shock resulting from a bullet wound. His sudden demise came as a devastating blow, and the community mourned his loss. But his dream did not die with him.

Puryear and others, including Black leader James A. R. Kinney, were successful in persuading the government to approve the proposal. About a month after Johnston's death, an act was passed to incorporate "The Nova Scotia Home for Colored Children." By 1917 the Home had its first Board of Trustees in place, made up of both Black and white members, including Henry G. Bauld as president, Reverend Puryear, J. A. R. Kinney, R. H. Murray of the Society for the Prevention of Cruelty, and nine others. The board's first task was to choose the location of the new institution. Originally, the board secured an abandoned building in the north end of Halifax that had once been a home for boys, and wasted no time in acquiring a grant from the city. The building was renovated, and soon after its first matron was hired: a woman from Philadelphia named Julia Jackson, whose time in Nova Scotia ended up being very short. Everything was set. Then, just as the official opening was about to take place, the second tragedy occurred: the biggest disaster to ever strike the City of Halifax.

On December 6, 1917, the weather was sunny and the skies were clear, but the biggest man-made explosion in the world was about to befall the small capital city. The *Mont Blanc*, a vessel carrying deadly cargo (picric acid, benzol, guncotton, and TNT) and initially headed for the war in France, left New York Harbor on December 1 to join a convoy in Halifax. At the same time, an empty Belgian relief supply ship, the *Imo*, sat in the Bedford

Basin. It was set to make its way to New York to collect emergency supplies. Neither ship would ever reach its destination. The *Mont Blanc* and *Imo* collided on that fateful day, causing a massive explosion in the harbour. Close to two thousand people died, with more in the days following. Nine thousand others suffered injuries, many of them quite serious. The explosion decimated the city's north end, abolished whole communities, families, and businesses, and left over six thousand people homeless. Among them were Black children. Among those businesses destroyed was the new site of the Home: the building was flattened. The Home would not come to fruition for another four years.

With nowhere to go, newly orphaned children wandered the streets destitute and alone. Immediately following the explosion, the city formed the Halifax Relief Commission, an emergency three-man committee tasked with administering a $30 million budget to fund reconstruction, social welfare, compensation, and medical care. As a result of the damages to north end Halifax as well as parts of Bedford and Dartmouth, social assistance organizations were bursting at the seams: they were over capacity and running out of supplies.

The increasing numbers of Black children needing help made it clear to the board that the Home's new accommodations would have to be much larger. R. H. Murray suggested to the Home's Board of Trustees that it try to find an area conducive to farming to ensure the children would have valuable resources like vegetables and livestock for eating and that they would learn valuable skills. In 1919 the City of Halifax acquired the MacKenzie property on Preston Road (now known as Main Street in Dartmouth) and deeded it to the Home. Although the goal of the Home had strayed from Johnston's initial vision of

NSA, HELEN CREIGHTON FONDS, 1987-178

The grand opening of the Nova Scotia Home for Colored Children, June 6, 1921.

an educational institution, the initial intent of creating a sanctuary for orphaned and neglected children would soon begin to take shape.

The sky was clear on June 6, 1921. Temperatures reached fifteen degrees Celsius. A sea of freshly pressed suits, hats, and vintage dresses swept through the grounds of the newly built Nova Scotia Home for Colored Children. It was a grand opening unlike any other. Said to be the largest gathering of Blacks in Nova Scotia since the arrival of Black Loyalists to Shelburne in 1783, over three thousand spectators looked on as dignitaries and leaders formed a procession that stretched over a kilometre. The event was heralded as one of the proudest moments for Nova Scotia's Black community. Reverend Puryear, Henry G. Bauld, James A. R. Kinney, and the others could finally reap the rewards of their hard work. The dream inspired by Johnston, who was gone too soon, had finally become a reality.

The original Nova Scotia Home for Colored Children, built in 1921.

Running the Home

After the excitement of the grand opening had passed, it was time to get down to the business of running the Home. In hindsight, it may have been doomed before it had a chance, starting with its hiring. Most of the staff put in charge of child care had little to no experience or training in dealing with children, not to mention children who were broken, had been neglected and abandoned, or at the very least were separated from their families. Coupled with this initial short-sightedness were the challenges and struggles of maintaining fiscal success without adequate funding. It wasn't long after the Home's opening that child welfare workers began to raise concerns.

On several occasions, officials from Nova Scotia's Department of Community Services visited the Home and made recommendations for further examination. For example, a 1948 child welfare visitation report compiled by Lilian Romkey and contained in the court documents provided by Mike Dull, included a profile of the Home's matron, in which she recorded the matron saying that the children were "poor trash" and that she hated the sound of them even talking. Because of her aversion, the matron said, she forbade them to talk at mealtime. As the children arrived from school during the questioning, Romkey noted the matron was extremely annoyed at the chatter. She also noted that the running of the Home was extremely and unnecessarily rigid. The welfare worker raised questions in her report as to how the Home's Board of Trustees, who admitted to being aware of the matron's ways, allowed her behaviour, and why the trustees would keep an employee on staff who so openly detested the children. Romkey also noted a complete absence of toys and games in both the girls' and boys' play areas and recommended that the Home provide the children with play equipment. There is nothing in provincial government records to suggest that any follow-up on the concerns noted in these types of reports ever took place.

That same year, various children's aid societies raised questions about the money being sent to the Home for its wards. At the time, Dr. Fred MacKinnon was fairly new in his role as the provincial director of Child Welfare. He'd become an advocate for Nova Scotia's poor and served as a political figure and public servant for over fifty years. He later had a hand in the Social Assistance Act of 1958 to decriminalize poverty and was inducted into the Order of Canada. In the late 1940s a letter from Margaret Payne, of Colchester County Children's Aid, landed on MacKinnon's desk. The department owed the Home family allowance money but was reluctant to send it. During that time, the wards received

Children play on handmade swings on the Home grounds. Residents spent most of their time outside.

allowances from their respective counties to take care of their needs, such as clothing and toys. Over six hundred dollars had accumulated in Colchester County alone, which rightfully belonged to its wards at the Home. That was a lot of money in 1948. However, Colchester expressed serious concerns about where and how the money was being spent. In her letter, Payne wrote, "We have corresponded with the Home on several occasions asking for suggestions or vouchers for things the children need but have had no satisfactory reply." She indicated that the Home's officials responded by insisting the money be turned over to them.

MacKinnon also received concerns from Walter Wood of Annapolis County Children's Aid. Wood wrote to MacKinnon in March of 1948, indicating that Mr. Bauld, superintendent of the Home, had demanded Wood's department send the family allowance money immediately. Wood stated in his letter, "There

"A sand box," one of the areas the children frequented for play.

is a large question in our minds as to what the money we hold in trust for these children has to do with the financing for the Nova Scotia Home for Colored Children, and we would be very glad to hear from you concerning the matter." Up until this point, Annapolis County had been paying five dollars a week per ward to the Home and holding the family allowance in trust. It's possible that the Home's board viewed this denial of funds as racially motivated red tape.

Meanwhile, some of the Children's Aid societies expressed mistrust for the Home's Board of Trustees and its distribution of funds. The records do not show the reasoning behind the funding being held was clearly communicated with the Home's officials. The ongoing denial of funds, coupled with MacKinnon's repeated denials for any increases in per diems for those wards living at the Home, contributed to the institution's already inadequate financial situation.

The bigger issue was not that child welfare agencies had concerns about money, but that government knew there were issues at the Home and was not addressing them. The continual requests from the Home for money were in part due to the fact that it received almost three times less per child than similar institutions in the province. In the Home's detailed 1974 brief to the Department of Social Services, the board's summary of requests included, "the leveling [sic] off of the per diem rate at a realistic figure in line with other specialized social service programs of this sort." It later summarized the board's request for ward support, staff training, and other issues by stating, "[T]he foregoing is support of our request that, in consideration of, and in preparation for an improved child development program for Black children in Nova Scotia, in improved facilities, with more expert staff, the Provincial Government support this program to a more realistic extent, starting initially with a grant structure to assist in a developmental financial platform."

The brief, which outlined initiatives to improve the organization of the Home and its care of the children, was one of many presented over decades to the Province of Nova Scotia. Letters sent from the Board of Trustees to the Department of Social Services suggest the Home was struggling financially and could not properly care for its wards with the scarce financial assistance the government provided. A letter from the Home to the Province in 1973 stated, "The amount of $3.50 is not sufficient. With the high cost of living, food, clothing, etc., it costs the Home nearly $9.00 per diem to care for each child."

Jane Earle, acting executive director of the Home in 1980, later indicated the Home had historically been "chronically underfunded." Wards in other similar institutions were receiving $9.00, and in provincial group homes and multifunctional models

$10.90 per diem. A 1973 handwritten note to the minister of Social Services outlined these figures. In her October 18, 2012, interview with the *Chronicle-Herald*, Earle stated the Home's per diem rates were not increased until 1976. A letter from MacKinnon to the Home dated July 15, 1976, confirmed his approval of a per diem increase to $14.30 after years of repeated requests. When Jane began working at the Home for free in 1980, per diems for the Home had been raised to $27.88, but by this time wards in other group homes were receiving $55.

The Home's staff members were also grossly underpaid. In her 1966 report, Rosemary Rippon, director of the Lunenburg County Children's Aid Society, stated, "There is some dissatisfaction among the staff regarding the wages paid, which are low and do not meet even the minimum wage scale."

MacKinnon and his staff were very involved in the financial affairs of the Home and more than half of the Home's funding came from MacKinnon's department. But they were aware of its shortcomings: lack of trained staff, stretched finances, and concerns of abuse. However, there are no records to indicate the Province made any significant changes. Conversely, records show some of the concerns that plagued the Home in its early years were still unresolved by the early 1970s.

A 1947 report completed by one of MacKinnon's staff documented that the Home had sixty children and only three regular staff, as two had quit and the Home's resident teacher was away for the summer. That same report described the Home's sleeping conditions and indicated that the girls' and boys' dorms were hugely overcrowded, with beds barely twenty inches apart. There was only one bathroom for each gender, and each had only one toilet with no seat cover.

NSA, BOB BROOKS FONDS, 1989-468

A child sitting down to a meal in the Home's later days.

A year after that report, MacKinnon, who oversaw the child welfare workers, paid a visit to the Home, along with one of his departmental employees, a Ms. Grandy, during the children's lunchtime routine. In his subsequent February 4, 1948, report he documented that there was "nothing on the table besides some fish chowder…there was no bread or butter or milk, either on the table or in evidence in the kitchen." He also noted that there was "too evident a contrast between the supervisor's [*sic*] rooms and the reception rooms, and the quarters in which the boys and girls are kept." Finally, he expressed concern that had he not shown up, the children, he was convinced, would have received nothing more than fish chowder with no fish.

However, despite his observations, there is no evidence to suggest MacKinnon ever followed up on improvements to the facility. Decades later, many of the same issues were still being documented. Even after receiving a detailed estimate of expenses for upgrades and renovations to the Home's living space, and despite multiple requests for additional funding, MacKinnon continually responded with a resounding *no*. The fact that the Province placed little value on the lives of the children who resided in the Home is a sad and stark reminder of the ugliness of racial injustice and discriminatory practices.

In her February 2012 affidavit to the courts, filed by Wagners as part of the class action suit, Child Welfare Consultant Sandra Scarth outlined evidence showing the Province had breached its duties and responsibilities to the former residents of the Home. In it, she cited specific examples of documented deficiencies over the years, which the Province knew about, including Home visits by government officials, after which they expressed and reported serious concerns.

One of those serious concerns was discussed following a 1954 incident involving a child named Sheila (last name witheld) who was removed from the Home and placed in a Halifax foster home. Upon arrival at her foster placement, the child had marks on her back and multiple bruises on her legs. The child told her new foster parents that she'd been beaten at the Home with a broomstick and switches. The foster parents in turn felt the matter was serious and needed to be dealt with right away. A. P. Hunt, executive director of the Yarmouth Children's Aid Society, wrote a scathing report to MacKinnon on the child's condition. According to the report, the little girl had also arrived at the foster home wearing a coat that was too small and too short. She had practically no underwear, and the few dresses she owned were all too short. The only nightdress she had was made out of an old flour bag. She'd also admitted to witnessing another little girl beaten so badly that she'd screamed for mercy. Staff had broken a broom handle over that child's back. Hunt stated in his letter, "As I have received several complaints about the children being abused and ill-treated at the Nova Scotia Home for Colored Children, I feel it is time that a thorough investigation was made as to what is going on there." He indicated that some of the reports also came from residents who had aged out of the system and from other foster parents who had received placements from the Home. In a follow-up letter, he urged again that MacKinnon's department conduct a thorough investigation. Despite his pleas on several occasions, however, no records suggest that MacKinnon initiated or conducted a thorough investigation into Mr. Hunt's concerns.

In turn, the Home's frequent requests for support were also repeatedly rejected. In his February 2012 affidavit to the courts, class action lawyer Mike Dull attached a document discussing the per diems the Home received from the Province. The provincial rate for institutions was set at $3.50/child in 1917. It wasn't until 1948, thirty-one years later, that the Home's rate would finally be increased. In another letter to the province dated January 5, 1959, the Home's Board requested additional funding, "in order for us to continue to meet the present day needs of the children entrusted to our care, not from the standpoint of increased numbers and expansion, but in order to achieve the child care standards as set forth by the Nova Scotia Department of Child Welfare, even if we had only half the number of fifty-five children now in residence." The response letter from MacKinnon, dated January 7, indicated the request was not granted. MacKinnon reasoned the government had numerous requests for funds and couldn't approve them all—even though this was an institution caring for the department's own wards.

In her 1966 report, Rosemary Rippon, coordinator of Foster Care Services in Nova Scotia, expressed deep concerns following an official visit to the Home. She noted the food kept in the Home's refrigerator was only sufficient for the staff and not enough to feed sixty-four children. She also indicated that none of the staff had formal training in child care or nursing.

Mr. MacKinnon responded with a letter to Mr. D. H. Johnson of the War Supplies Agency Center in Ontario, attaching the report and suggesting, "One of the first things we should do is to arrange for a meeting with the societies boarding children at the Nova Scotia Home for Colored Children. The facts of life pertaining to these children, the arrangements being made, or shall I say the lack of satisfactory arrangements, will have to be discussed very frankly." There are no records to indicate whether such a meeting ever transpired or whether any significant change was made to improve the care of the children as a result of the report.

Numerous records indicate the Province was aware of issues and complaints regarding the Home but did not act upon them and, as a result, neglected to protect the wards in its care. D. H. Johnson, who had moved to a position in Family and Child Welfare, sent a letter to the minister of Public Welfare, William Gillis, dated June 13, 1972, to inform him that the Home was considering conducting an assessment and revising its program to better meet the needs of the children. This assessment would include an evaluation of how the Home was being run, the competence and training of staff, and funding. The initial estimate for such an assessment was $1,500. Consultant Ernest Rafuse later projected a cost of $4,000 for his firm to complete an in-depth assessment. (One can only imagine what it could have uncovered.)

In his response letter, dated June 19, the minister advised Johnson that he would not authorize the expense.

Lawyer Mike Dull also attached private interdepartmental correspondence, dated March 8, 1973, to his affidavit. It referenced the proposed evaluation and contained a handwritten note cautioning against the study, citing that it would be no more than a "witch hunt" at the expense of the department. Subsequent documents show how Johnson and others, such as J. A. MacKenzie, warned Deputy Minister MacKinnon not to get involved with funding the Home's assessment. In one such note, Mr. MacKenzie is quoted as saying, "to fund such a study is simply paying for a stick to beat ourselves."

In his subsequent letter to the minister, Mr. MacKinnon cited his agreement with the warnings, further stating, "if we do not permit ourselves to get involved, we will then be in a position to defend ourselves if the Home goes ahead with the study and undertakes the usual muck-raking and mud-slinging which is characteristic of this kind of effort where Government is concerned."

Later that year, in response to the Home's ongoing plea to the Province for increased per diems, and despite the Province's arm's-length approach to funding a study into the Home's operations, Mr. Johnson suggested to Mr. MacKinnon that, "The per diem paid for wards at the Nova Scotia Home for Colored Children should not be increased until such time as the Home has established a satisfactory program." Just as unfortunate was Mr. MacKinnon's private written response to Johnson, further demonstrating that the Province's focus was its own agenda rather than the safety and well-being of the children. While Mr. MacKinnon agreed that the Home should not keep asking for funds, he stated, "to deny them the money would simply create the impression that we are being negative and using that back door method of vetoing the project. I would suggest to you that while we may have misgivings we will do great harm to the Department by taking that line at the moment...[providing the NSHCC with financing] is an investment in public relations which if not met would put this Department in a very bad light."

What We Have Learned

While government officials dodged important opportunities to support the residents or to investigate and prevent the continued abuses at the Home, the children suffered in silence. Many female former residents who lived there during the 1970s shared similar stories of certain male staff who were always too willing to drive them to their weekend hangout spot—but there was always a catch: straws were drawn and whoever got the shortest straw had to "put out" as payment for the free transportation. Trips in the car for "ice cream" were also common, as were stories of male staff getting young girls pregnant. According to the girls, like Harriet, who later shares her story, these instances were swept under the rug.

In her affidavit to the courts, Deanna Smith recalled her roommate crying as she wrote incidents in her diary, and that staff found the diary and destroyed its pages. Over the years, dating back to the early beginnings of the Home, many alleged that pregnant girls who fell ill were sent to a "sick" room to rest. No rest was had. They recounted stories of staff entering the sick room and fondling them. In some cases they were raped.

A child recites a prayer before mealtime.

Countless former residents also alleged that if a baby died, it was buried in the woods behind the Home. While this has not been proven, multiple former residents, many of whom do not even know each other, have mentioned it. One former resident lay in hospital after being hit by a car. In this book, she recounts the story of her visits by a male staff member who violated her sexually as she tried to recover. Incidents like these, which we have seen occur over and over again throughout history, demonstrate that we have more work to do as a society.

The boards presiding over the Home had a duty to provide good leadership. Despite staunch efforts over time, gaps in care and safety still managed to form, and efforts sometimes fell short of providing for the best interests of the children under its care. Reverend Dr. W. P. Oliver wrote about the Home in a 1971 report, crediting one of its first board members, J. A. R. Kinney. He describes Kinney as one of the most highly trained and exceptional Black Nova Scotia leaders of his time and the guiding force behind the Home's legacy. Records also show that at one point, Mr. Kinney, during his leadership of the board, demanded and instituted a strict "no corporal punishment" rule for the Home. In one case, when it was brought to Mr. Kinney's attention that a child had been severely scarred as a result of a beating, Kinney fired the staff member responsible.

Other dedicated board members and staff also served the Home over the years, but unfortunately, in many cases, the culture of secrecy among them was so deeply entrenched that even those board members with the best of intentions couldn't break through the staff's code of silence. When it came to the Home, there was a "hear no evil, see no evil" mindset: What you saw, you didn't really see. What you heard, you didn't really hear. And what was done to you, never really happened.

For much of the Home's operation, society, aware of frequent abuses behind closed doors in many homes, believed that what happened inside a person's home was nobody's business. Many religious families believed that according to the Bible it was the woman's duty to be subservient to her husband. As a result, many wives who were abused simply suffered in silence. Children received harsh and severe treatment both in school and at home. People knew, but no one confronted the abusers.

Still, incidents at the Home became so well known and so often spoken about that people in the community would use them to make idle threats to their kids. When their children misbehaved, parents would say, "If you keep acting out, I will put you in the Home." The threat alone was often enough to make children pause and obey. This attests to the fact that even in the Home's early days, the community believed the treatment of the children living there was suspect. However, having knowledge and acting on it are two very different things. Firstly, most community members wouldn't have known where to begin to challenge an establishment with such a praiseworthy status. They risked being seen as disturbers, outliers who didn't support the cause. Secondly, in those times, many were also experiencing, inflicting, and/or witnessing abuses in their own homes and understood the shame associated with having others know what was going on behind closed doors.

But what about the absent social workers whose job it was to protect the children? How did the plight of these children fall upon deaf ears and blind eyes? With dark clouds of secrecy and shame looming, what were these abandoned children to do? Where could they possibly turn? Although some were fortunate to be taken into a loving foster home, regrettably, the way out for most children throughout the history of the Home, and particularly prior to the 1970s, involved either running away or aging out of the system.

Fortunately, out of tragedy often come new lessons. From society's inability to protect its children came stronger policies with greater surveillance and sweeping changes to the practice of social work that have thrust the best interests of the child to the forefront. While the system still has its flaws, we as a society now possess the insight and initiative to ensure it is working for our children.

We now know that certain factors increase a child's risk of abuse. These include the child's level of vulnerability and quality of supervision and protection. We understand as a society that a child's environment and circumstances can make a child more vulnerable to abuse. In the case of the Home, inadequate staff training in some cases, along with separation from parents, emotional vulnerability, and lack of supervision by social service officials, all served as potential factors that contributed to the negative experiences of many residents: a recipe that brewed the scandal that has tarnished the Home's once extraordinary reputation.

In 1985 Dr. Christopher Bagley, professor at the University of Calgary, and his associate, Richard Ramsey, conducted a community mental health study using a sample of 377 women from a large Canadian city in order to identify a correlation between childhood sexual abuse and increased incidence of mental health issues in adult survivors. This resulted in an increased awareness of systemic abuse of children in Nova Scotia in what was known as the Bagley report, where it was noted that biases associated with sexual abuse were disappearing and greater attentiveness to the issue was beginning to surface.

Twenty-two per cent of the women surveyed admitted to experiencing abuse as a child, and these women were twice as likely to present with some form of mental health challenge. The study also examined implications for social work practice. It began to raise flags in the social work community, prompting professionals to further examine this issue of childhood abuse and its effects on the children as they reach adulthood.

When the report was published, it was believed that 18 to 30 per cent of women had experienced some form of unwanted sexual interference at some point in their lives. Today, thanks to research by Lucie Ogrodnik, manager of Statistics Canada's Family Violence Program, we know that possibly one-third of the population has experienced child abuse; 81 per cent of physical assaults against children under six reported to police were committed by someone who the child knew; and for every ten of them, six were perpetrated by a family member or person acting as a parent/guardian (Ogrodnik, 2010). Female children are more likely to be victims of family violence than their male counterparts, a finding that Ogrodnik suggests is largely driven by the numbers of sexual offence victimizations of girls. For example, in 2009 girls under the age of eighteen were over four times more likely to be sexually assaulted by a family member than boys of the same age.

Current statistics on childhood sexual abuse can only estimate the unreported cases. A true estimation would see the numbers skyrocket. It is when we begin to look at the numbers and unpack the findings that a clearer picture begins to emerge, such as the realities of the long-term effects that victims carry into adulthood. There continue to be high numbers of undocumented, unreported cases of abuse in our communities. The goal for practitioners is to continually work to identify what can further be done to protect children from harm.

Chapter 3

Coming Forward

"ME AND MY FOUR SIBLINGS and one other child were the only white kids at the Home at that time," read former resident Shirley Melanson's affidavit filed during the class action suit. She had been snatched from her home in 1947 without explanation and driven to the institution by a social worker. "In the mornings after the residents ate breakfast, we were put outside in the open air without adequate clothing and were made to stay outside until the next mealtime. We were very cold and sometimes we were forced to stay out there in subzero temperature[s]."

She wasn't the only one to make such claims. Others have come forward to tell how they nearly froze as they stood outside for hours, cold and hungry, and resorted to eating whatever food they could find.

"I watched my brother get beaten with the buckle of a belt. His back was full of blood and his body full of welts. My sister used to wet the bed and was made to sleep in her wet sheets. She got beaten with a strap every time she wet the bed, which happened on an almost daily basis," said Shirley, who left the

The entrance to the Nova Scotia Home for Colored children on Main Street in Westphal.

home in 1948. On one occasion, she was so upset watching the staff member beat her sister that she bit the woman on the back of the leg. The staff member threw her down the stairs, causing the resident to break her arm. She wasn't taken to a doctor. Her arm was in a sling when the social worker showed up. She told him what happened and showed him the stairs she'd been thrown down, hoping he would get her and her siblings out of the Home. The Home staff member convinced the social worker the resident had fallen down the stairs.

Clark Cromwell was placed in the Home as a baby and lived there until 1951, when he was nine. "This scar under my chin, this happened when I was five. One of the women threw me over the bannister and I split my chin open and had to get stitches," he recounted similarly to a Halifax *Chronicle-Herald* reporter in a 2012 interview. "They starved us kids. I remember being so hungry we would throw rocks at the pigs so we could get to their food and eat it."

In the early 1990s many others began to reveal the horrors they suffered as children growing up in the Nova Scotia Home for Colored Children. One of them was Peter Smith. By 1998 Peter decided he would write a book to share his story with the world. He wanted people to know what happened to him and the other children in the Home. He wrote a letter to Oprah Winfrey, asking her for help to tell his story. That fall, her representatives responded by letter saying they were unable to help but wished him the best in his endeavour. Imagine what may have happened had the talk show host responded in his favour. Before contacting Oprah, between expenses related to contacting former residents who lived far away and purchasing recording equipment to gather the stories, Peter had already exceeded his limited budget. Eventually, he became ill and was unable to pursue his dream, although he retained his desire to let the world know the stories he'd collected. He passed all of his information on to his brother Garnet, who tells his own story in Chapter 5.

Tony Smith, another former resident, began documenting his experiences almost ten years prior to Peter. He, too, wanted to write a book and, in the early 1990s, approached Charles R. Saunders about it. Unfortunately, nothing materialized beyond their original discussion. Had Tony succeeded, not only would his book have become one of the first to document the deep-seated abuses that had occurred at the Home, but it may have equally served as encouragement to help others come forward sooner and bring about a speedier conclusion to what became a decade-long court battle.

Dull and firm owner Ray Wagner, the class action lawyers who eventually won compensation for the Home's former residents, had been championing their cause from the outset, well before the public became aware of their fight. In March 2001 Wagners law firm launched legal action against the Home, the Attorney General, and the Children's Aid Society and Family Services of Colchester County on behalf of former resident Robert Borden. In May 2002 Ottawa lawyers also launched legal action against the Home, the Attorney General, and the Halifax Children's Aid Society on behalf of Tony Smith. These actions alleged various government agencies were vicariously liable for physical and sexual assault, negligence, and breach of fiduciary duty. In both cases, the Home and Children's Aid applied for a summary judgment to have all claims dismissed, arguing that the statute of limitations had run out. Until the statute of limitations was eliminated in 2014, statute on sexual assault was only for one year.

It is ironic that the Children's Aid Society positioned itself in opposition to these abuse victims while, as a representative for the Province, it had the legal obligation to protect the children in its care; it had failed to do so in both cases and should have seized the opportunity presented by both lawsuits to re-examine policies and improve the quality of protection for children in its care. Instead, it contested. In both cases, all actions filed on behalf of both men were dismissed in 2009.

In April 2010, appeals subsequently filed on behalf of both plaintiffs were unsuccessful. Motions for reconsideration were filed in November of the same year. Finally, in January 2011, the Supreme Court of Canada accepted the motion for reconsideration. About a month later, the Home, Children's Aid, and the Attorney General filed responses, requesting that the motion for reconsideration be dismissed with costs, which would mean former residents who had brought the suit against the Home and the Province would have to pay all costs incurred for their defence, adding to the many burdens former residents would have to endure.

That same February, Wagner and Associates filed a Notice of Action and Statement of Claim with the courts on behalf of Aubrey Pelley and Deanna Smith, who would serve as lead plaintiffs. The intent was to commence a proposed Class Proceeding in the Supreme Court of Nova Scotia against the Nova Scotia Home for Colored Children and the Attorney General of Nova Scotia. Their Statement of Claim alleged the abuses were systemic in nature: "During all relevant years, the Defendant [The Nova Scotia Home for Colored Children] operated, caused to be operated, or permitted to be operated a residential facility whose residents were systemically subject to abuse and mistreatment," the proposed class action stated. It also alleged the Home "created an atmosphere of indifference, tolerance and encouragement of excessive mental, physical and sexual abuse such that the repugnant practices pervaded the NSHCC and the relationships between the residents of the NSHCC as well as between the agents, employees, servants and residents of the NSHCC."

In April 2011 the Supreme Court of Canada dismissed the motions for reconsideration filed on behalf of Robert Borden and Tony Smith with costs. It was another crushing defeat, and few media outlets picked up bits and pieces of the story. Despite the loss, the Class Proceedings filed on behalf of Pelly and Smith continued. In June 2011 the courts stamped an order appointing Justice Arthur LeBlanc as case management judge. A case management conference was held in December of that year, and a timetable that spanned 2012 was set aside for proceedings, including five days in October for the Certification motion to be heard before the courts.

In January of 2013 the Home's executive director, Veronica Marsman, filed an affidavit on its behalf. In it, she stated, "I am informed by counsel for the Home and do believe, that in the individual actions, the following former residents of the Home have been accused of sexual, physical or mental abuse by plaintiffs in those actions." She went on to name fifty-nine former residents, many of whom were a part of the class action suit, whose members alleged that they were abused by staff, including VOICES leader, Tracy Dorrington, along with Robert Borden, whose individual law suit against the Home and the province was dismissed in 2009. The affidavit went on to say that to Marsman's knowledge, the ED was only aware of one staff member who had sexual contact with a resident. The affidavit was a crushing blow to those former residents who had been seriously abused and mistreated. Former resident Tony Smith, also a leader of VOICES, publicly called it an attempt by lawyers to turn the focus on residents as *perpetrators* and not as victims themselves.

Meanwhile, in February 2013, the class action order was amended to remove Pelly's name as plaintiff and add former residents June Elwin and Harriet Johnson as plaintiffs, along with Deanna Smith. The order continued to allege, among many other things, that the Home failed to hire trained workers as was standard in other institutions; failed to investigate, evaluate, or monitor the quality of care of the residents; inappropriately and inadequately responded, investigated, or inquired into complaints of physical, mental, and sexual abuse that the Home knew or ought to have known of; and chose not to identify the need for or provide necessary medical, psychological, and psychiatric treatments. The Attorney General subsequently filed a motion with the court to strike all or portions of many of the affidavits filed by former residents, social workers, and experts for the plaintiffs. The evidence in support of the motion was based on an affidavit sworn by Beverly MacDonald, a child welfare specialist from Pictou County, Nova Scotia. In its June 26 decision, the court struck out a few portions of certain affidavits, such as specific statements deemed irrelevant, and allowed the rest to remain. In essence, the plaintiffs were ordered to revise some of the affidavits to exclude the agreed upon statements.

Over 140 former residents who lived at the Home between 1941 and 1986 eventually signed on to the proposed class action lawsuit. In it, former residents sought acknowledgement from the Province of Nova Scotia that they had not received the protection they deserved as children. After word spread about the impending suit, the province's Black community quickly became divided. Many were shocked and saddened. Others were angry and confused. Many were unsure as to whether anything had really happened to the Home's former residents.

However, Wagners's team of lawyers uncovered documented evidence that serious abuse had occurred. They also uncovered medical records indicating an unreported rape and others that showed officials were aware of concerns regarding the safety and welfare of the children, but did little to address them. Even recommendations for investigations made to the government by its own workers were largely ignored, the lawyers alleged. Dull, the law firm's representative, suggested complaints went unaddressed because it was easier for the government to pretend they never happened than to have an issue come back on them down the road, the document said.

Children spent time in a common area that reportedly contained little to no toys or games to stimulate them.

An affidavit filed by Mike Dull at Wagners describes the sexual abuse of children by staff members in the Home as "pandemic." It also describes verbal abuses, such as the children being called "nigger, stupid, and useless." Beatings were a regular occurrence there and many children suffered from malnutrition. Dull reported that the Home had become a "dumping ground" and that the children living there suffered in silence.

In 2012 Victor Lewin, a paralegal at Wagners, laid out a stark comparison between how the government handled two very similar institutional abuse allegations. In his blog for the law firm, Lewin listed the similarities between the Home (mostly Black children) and the Shelburne Home for Boys (mostly white children). Both institutions opened in the 1920s and were funded by the Province of Nova Scotia (although the Home's subsidies were not equal to those of other government-funded institutions). Both used unqualified staff and were subsequently subject to severe abuse allegations. But he points out that the government's handling of the allegations were anything but similar. The Province immediately jumped to provide funding for a complete investigation after former Shelburne residents came forward with claims of abuse. Within five years of the first allegations, the government had provided full compensation to Shelburne's victims and charges were brought against those who committed the abusive acts. In the case of the Nova Scotia Home for Colored Children, however, no inquiries into similar allegations were ever made. No abuser was ever charged. No money was ever provided for an investigation, said Lewin. And more than ten years after the very first motion was filed with the courts in 2001, former residents were still fighting for the Province to even acknowledge their experiences. In fact, much of the litigation involved the Home's and the Province's repeated applications to the court to block proceedings and dismiss the claims of residents on the basis that they should have come forward with their allegations sooner.

Throughout the remainder of 2013, various amended statements and new evidence were filed with the courts. In the meantime, the Nova Scotia Home for Colored Children decided to settle with the plaintiffs for $5 million. Because of this settlement, the Home was not a part of Justice LeBlanc's ninety-eight-page Supreme Court decision in December 2013 greenlighting the class action but the certification of the motion was a victory for former residents.

In June of 2014, Wagners entered into a settlement agreement with the Province of Nova Scotia on behalf of the Home's former residents, eliminating the need to call numerous witnesses to testify during the class action proceedings and relive the most traumatic experiences of their lives. Former residents would finally receive justice and compensation. The Province agreed to settle for $29 million, to be added to the Home's previous settlement of $5 million.

By the summer of 2015, all of those former residents who had signed on to the class action and were deemed eligible had received their compensation. But there was one thing still missing. Former residents still longed for a public apology from the Home, acknowledging the pain and trauma they had suffered there as children. The Home remained silent, as it did a year before, when Nova Scotia premier Stephen McNeil issued a public apology on behalf of the Province. As residents came forward, one after another, to share their pain publicly, the Home still chose to remain silent. It was an appalling rejection for the Home's former residents who had suffered at the hands of staff.

It wasn't until the Province held a small press conference to announce details about the restorative inquiry beginning in the fall of 2015 that a Home representative gave a brief statement apologizing to former residents for what they endured as children. The apology was met with tears by some of those in attendance. It was what they had been waiting all these years to hear.

Chapter 4

Harriet

HARRIET JOHNSON WAS RAISED BY her grandparents from birth. She was about eight years old when her grandmother passed away in 1976. Her grandfather became unable to care for Harriet and her cousin due to issues with alcohol, and about a year later, she and her cousin Russell became wards of the court. They were driven almost two hours away from their grandparents' house in New Glasgow to the Nova Scotia Home. Harriet describes the social worker who took them away as a short white woman who walked with a limp. After she dropped Harriet and her cousin off at the Home, Harriet says they never saw her again.

Harriet was just eleven when she experienced a disturbing sexual encounter with one of the Home's staff members. In her affadavit filed with the courts during the class action suit against the Home and the Province of Nova Scotia, Harriet bravely shared one of the most harrowing and traumatic experiences of her life.

During evening rounds, two male staff members would enter my bedroom and close the door. They would sit by my bed, place their hands under the sheets and rub my breasts and buttocks. This occurred every night when they were on duty. One afternoon I went for a drive with one of them. We were in a white car with a white leather interior. I do not recall where we planned on going; he drove us around the entirety of the junior high school. There was no one present. He then drove to the back of the school and parked his car. He told me to get into the back seat. I did so. When I was in the back seat, he moved the front seats up. He got out of the car and joined me in the back seat.

When both of us were in the back seat, he pushed me to the ground. He pressed on my back as he pulled down my pants and underwear. He then raped me from behind. For a very long time he penetrated my vagina and anus, going back and forth between each. I recall that he had one hand on both butt cheeks and that he forcibly spread them apart as he raped me. I was in an incredible amount of pain. I screamed and screamed. I begged and yelled at the top of my lungs for him to stop. He did not.

I was soon covered in my own blood but he continued. He continued to rape me while I was pinned to the ground on my stomach until he eventually ejaculated. I was not older than eleven when I was raped in this fashion. This was my first sexual encounter. I was a virgin before this rape. After he ejaculated and stopped raping me, he told me to pull up my underwear and pants and return to the front seat. I was bleeding from my vagina and anus. There was blood everywhere. In shock, I did as I was told and returned to the front seat. He warned me not to say anything about what happened to anyone.

When he drove me back to the Home, he told me to go straight to my room and stay there for the entire night. I was still bleeding so I did as I was told. I was scared of him. I did not tell anyone what he did to me.

"Harriet did not receive any medical attention following her experience," read an affadavit. It went on in detail:

She did get medical attention for a gash over her eye that she received during a beating from another male staff member, because it wouldn't stop bleeding. He told the doctor she ran into something. Harriet still has the scar above her eye as a reminder. Harriet remained a victim of repeated sexual and physical abuse, and claimed that the sexual acts went beyond staff and residents. She recalled walking into a room and witnessing two male and female staff members having sex with each other while on duty. She vividly remembers seeing the female staff's breasts. Harriet stated that staff was aware of everything that was going on. One white staff member pulled her aside and scolded her in relation to the male staff who had previously raped her. She told Harriet to stop kissing him on the lips. Harriet asserts that it was he who kept kissing her sexually in the mouth. She was the child.

Once she was finally old enough to leave the Home, at age fourteen, Harriet was tracked down by that same staff member who allegedly raped her again. In explosive court documents, Johnson claimed he then forced her into a life of prostitution, forcing her to endure two years of physical, sexual, and emotional pain and suffering. Many of the female former residents have alleged in court documents that the Home became a recruiting ground for pimps and sexual predators.

"When I was approximately sixteen, a travelling circus came to Halifax," says Harriet. She saw this as a way to escape from her pimp, that male staff member. "I joined up with the circus and they took me to Moncton. I was finally able to stop prostituting."

Harriet Johnson was a ward of the Province. The Province was supposed to protect her.

An internal Community Services welfare report completed on Harriet showed that workers were aware of her involvement with prostitution at a young age.

The dates coincide with the period of Harriet's claim that a male staff member forced her into the trade. The report, filed in 1988 at the Children's Aid Society of Pictou, documents Harriet's activities dating back to the late 1970s. Yet there is no documentation to suggest that social workers filed any incident reports of misconduct by the Home's staff.

During her two years away from the Home—when she was still a ward of the court—Harriet remembers asking herself why no social worker ever came looking for her. She believed that the Province didn't even know she had been taken away from the Home because no one ever showed up. Had a social worker done what they were expected to, her life may have taken a different turn. She may not have spent so many dark years living at the mercy of her perpetrator. That is the case for all of the former residents who suffered harm: had their social workers really carried out the visits they described in their falsified notes, many children would have been spared the pain of abuse.

Chapter 5

Garnet

"*SEEING IS BELIEVING.* **THAT'S WHAT** I would have called my book, if I was a writer," says Garnet. Tall but unassuming, the seventy-six-year-old has a welcoming smile. He is forthcoming and genuine in his delivery, and wants the world to know what has suffered. Over the years, Garnet has collected dozens of photographs, articles, and reports related to the Home. His meticulously documented collection, neatly stored in binders and boxes, is tucked away in a safe area of his cozy apartment. He wanted to write a book to tell the world his powerful story, but what most people don't know about Garnet is that he left the Home after thirteen years, unable to read or write.

When he and four of his seven siblings—three brothers and one sister—arrived at the Home in 1941, Garnet was just four years old. Once he reached five, he attended the Henry G. Bauld Center, the two-room school located on the Home's property. It was here he was supposed to receive his fundamental learning; however, even in education, his caregivers failed. "If you were a slow learner, you fell behind. There was no help." He leans forward in his chair when he speaks, then back again. "By the time I left the Home, I was almost seventeen and they put me in foster care until I was nineteen. I never got what I needed to succeed. They robbed me of my education. So I had to do what I had to do to survive."

By the time he was an adult, Garnet had perfected clever ploys to cover up the secret that he couldn't read or write. "I carried a sling with me whenever I knew

BONNIE WILLIAMS

Garnet recounts his courageous story.

I would be in a situation where I would have to write or sign my name," he says. "When someone asked me to write, I would show them my arm and pretend it was injured so I wouldn't have to write. Most times someone else would just do it for me." When it came to reading, Garnet would pat his pockets and say that he forgot his glasses—which he didn't even wear. He frequented a local restaurant, and because he couldn't read the menu, would always order the same thing: a hotdog. "I ate many hotdogs over the years," he admits.

On one particular visit, Garnet ordered his usual $1.49 hotdog but paid with a ten-dollar bill. The waitress did not bring him any change and he didn't ask for it. "It seemed like she had figured out that I couldn't read the menu and just ripped me off," he explains. "Then I decided I couldn't continue on that way anymore."

As a young man out in the world and far away from the Home, Garnet began to realize that he couldn't get by without knowing how to read and write. He was well into his twenties by the time he started teaching himself to read. He would memorize words by sight when someone read aloud from printed material. He would read signs on the street. He was diligent in his efforts to capture what he never learned as a child at the Home. Today, if he comes across a word he isn't sure of, he will stop and look it up to find its pronunciation and meaning. He continues to display true tenacity in handling the cards he was dealt.

Long before the more recent stories of abuse surfaced from the 1970s and later, children like Garnet had survived horrific abuses dating back as far as the 1930s and '40s. Education wasn't the only thing Garnet was robbed of. Nor was it the only secret he held in for so many years.

During our interview, Garnet sits up straight in his chair. He has a long story to tell. With a quiet, humble spirit and with eloquent speech, he continues to lay out for me the crucial moments that shaped his life.

Garnet was born in Weymouth, Nova Scotia, to a very young single mother who had five small children and no father to help. Eventually there would be eight siblings altogether—three with a different last name.

"Back in those days, people frowned upon women who had children out of wedlock," says Garnet. "I think my mother did what she could with what little she had, but she was also trying to survive herself. As children, we were constantly in the streets begging for something to eat. Finally, neighbours got fed up with us asking around for food and made a call to child welfare."

Digby Poorhouse, 1891–1963.

That phone call changed everything for Garnet and his siblings. "It was 1939. I was only about four years old," he recalls. "Me and my brothers and sister were snatched from our home by a child welfare worker: Peter, Gordon, Edgar, Mabel, and me. The older ones remember that our mother was watching while the worker forced them into the car. The worker dropped us off at the Poorhouse."

"The Poorhouse," as locals referred to it, was the Marshalltown poorhouse, technically named the Alms House, in Digby County, Nova Scotia. Built in 1891, it took in single mothers, children, and the mentally ill; a dumping ground for the unwanted. As with other institutions of its kind in Nova Scotia at that time, there were stories of abuse and neglect occurring there. Just two weeks after their arrival, on a drizzly night, Garnet and his brothers were taken from the Poorhouse and tossed into a Jeep. They were dropped off at the Home. The boys were immediately separated from their only sister, and there was little to no effort to keep families together. As a result, Garnet and his younger brothers didn't even realize their sister, Mabel, was related to them until years after they had all left the Home.

Garnet experienced many of the same emotions as other residents when he tried to piece together the puzzle of his childhood.

When I got the records of my time at the Home, I was hoping to get answers, but the information I wanted to know about most wasn't there. The department didn't have any solid records either. To this day, I still have no idea who took us away from our life in Weymouth. I do recall that some of the girls in the Home destroyed some of the records. They were being treated very badly, so one day they set fire to a file cabinet to get back at staff.

One of the residents involved in that incident corroborated that she and a few other girls rebelled against the staff, broke into an office that held most of the files, and deliberately set them on fire. Their anger was directed at staff, and they did not realize some of the files likely contained important records for residents. That resident recounts her powerful story later in this book.

Garnet's memory kicks in vividly just before he began his schooling. "I remember that time well because that's when the abuse started," he says.

Staff used to announce that they were checking under the blankets for wet beds, but their hands were always wandering under the blankets, longer than just checking for a wet bed. Then you would feel their hands touching your private areas. Even if you were asleep. Sometimes we would tell them that our beds were dry so they wouldn't check, but it didn't matter. Even though they knew the bed was dry their hands would still be under the blankets, molesting the children. And they made us wear bedclothes made out of short flour bags. It looked like a nightdress. The sack was so short and it would ride up on you when you moved around in bed.

As Garnet got older, his responsibilities increased. So did the abuse, which now included the rigorous physical labour involved in working the fields on the Home's property. While chores are seen as routine in many homes, Garnet and other former residents of the Home repeatedly describe their work as equivalent to severe child labour. They picked vegetables in the garden for extensive hours. When staff wasn't watching, the children would sneak and eat the peas because they were so hungry. If they got caught they knew they would receive a beating—no matter how hungry they were. A wagon would then take them further out, where they were then instructed to continue their work. On his first wagon ride, Garnet was under the impression he was going for an ice cream. But what he found was many rows of potatoes that had to be pulled from the ground.

"The Home also had livestock, hens, chickens, and pigs," explains Garnet. "They sent us kids in to collect the eggs from the barn. That barn was full of methane gas. We had no masks and no protection. We were forced to go inside, inhaling that gas while the farmhands stood outside and watched us."

Though there seemed to be food available, Garnet and others growing up in the Home experienced a constant feeling of hunger. "We were always hungry," he laughs, remembering.

"Every morning, breakfast was a bowl of powdered milk with a few dozen cornflakes sprinkled on top. Then in the cold months, it was oatmeal. Dinner was so predictable that we made up a song about it and we used to sing it all the time: *Boiled dinner; beans and potatoes; fish and potatoes; soup!*"

Garnet also remembers clearly a truck that used to arrive at the Home every Wednesday, loaded with restaurant leftovers and day-old food for the pigs: "Me and some of the other boys in the Home would watch the truck load the food into barrels. When the coast was clear, we would grab what we could and stash it in canvas bags. We would hide our stash at the back of the property under a tree. And every chance we got, we would sneak back to the tree and eat the food in the bags." It was what farmers called "slop," he says. Not fit for humans to eat.

Eventually, Garnet and the others noticed that when they returned to that tree, some food was missing. They later discovered the female residents had caught on to their stash and were also sneaking back to eat what the boys had stolen. When they were really hungry and food was very scarce, Garnet would eat the clovers that grew in the field. He would also eat whatever berries he could find, not certain if they were safe. He ate weeds that he said looked like green plants with little peas growing on them. He had no idea what they were; he just knew he needed to fill his stomach. As an adult, Garnet recalls never really getting sick much. He jokingly attributes that to all of the germs and dirt he ate as a child growing up in the Home.

Outside of the sparse breakfast and dinners the children received, there was nothing else. They weren't permitted snacks in between the meals that barely satisfied them, unless a child was a staff favourite. With the school located on the property, there were few outside eyes to see how much the children were actually being fed.

On soup days, the children complained because the broth didn't have any chicken. When bread was included, it was only one piece. The soup that Garnet referred to was also the subject of a 1948 report completed by Lillian Romkey, a social worker who visited the Home on several occasions. She was there during two separate mealtimes. In her report, she expressed concerns about the children being served soup consisting of only boiled water and chunks of potatoes and turnips. She was also concerned about the fish and potato meal. It was fish chowder with no fish: simply milk, potatoes, and a bunch of fish bones. During one visit, the children received the chowder with bones in it while the staff ate fried halibut, Romkey said.

While few outside knew what was happening at the home, people had knowledge that something wasn't right. These included government officials, community members, relatives, and those staff members who were not inflicting harm on the children but had witnessed others do so.

"The part I don't understand," Garnet says, "is that lots of parents in the surrounding communities knew that we were being mistreated. There were even relatives of some of us children who knew there was abuse but didn't reach out to help."

The abuse Garnet suffered only escalated as his body began to develop. The layout of the sleeping quarters was such that the boys were on one side and the girls on the other. A female staff member, Mrs. Jefferson—named multiple times throughout the court affidavits—would work during the night. Some of the male former residents use terms like "twisted" or "perverted" when referring to her. Garnet remembers clearly the woman's nightly ritual on the boys' side:

> She would wear long bloomers—that's what they were called back then—but she would cut big slits in the crotch area. At bedtime, she would sit at the top of the stairs with her legs wide open. We had to line up at the bottom of the stairs to brush our teeth—with one toothbrush. Then when we got to the top of the stairs, each one of us would have to stop and touch her private parts with our mouth before she would let us pass and go to bed. If we didn't do it to her liking, she would grab the back of our heads and press it down between her legs until we did it right. And we couldn't say no or we would get beaten.

Countless former residents have shared similar vivid memories of this woman and the abuses she inflicted.

Some residents, including Garnet, also described a room designated for punishment. If staff said you were getting a beating, most likely they would take you there. Except when that beating was administered by the woman who sat at the top of the stairs, the "beating" transformed into a sexual act. "Once you were inside that room for your punishment, she would whack the belt against the desk a few times and tell you to pretend to cry," says Garnet. "The crying was so that others would think you were being strapped, but what was really going on was that she would be forcing you to perform oral sex acts on her." He also remembers being taken downstairs to the farmhand by the same female staff member on many occasions. Once he got there, he would be made to perform oral sex on the male farmhand while the female staff member watched. (The relationship between the female staff member and farmhand remains unclear.)

A recurring negative theme tied to the staff's treatment of the children, say former residents, is the darker skinned you were, the worse you were treated. That doesn't negate the experiences of those children who were lighter skinned and still experienced abuse. Nor does it take away from the children who were dark but claim no harm came to them. But in society, there existed the ongoing dark-versus-light-skin issue within the Black community that many outside the race may not be aware of. The issues stem from the days of slavery in North America, when lighter-skinned or biracial slaves usually received better treatment and worked in the main house rather than in the hot sun all day. And if light enough, they could pass for white if it meant they could escape the harsh treatment other Blacks were experiencing. For some darker-skinned people, these realities caused resentment to build towards lighter-skinned Blacks; they cited favouritism and accused them of not being "Black" enough. For lighter-skinned Blacks and biracial people, it was often a matter of not feeling like they fit in: too light to be Black and too dark to be white. Again, not all Black people share these sentiments, but these are the foundation of the light-skinned/dark-skinned debate, which is still very much a controversial issue within society.

As it related to the Home, some former residents felt that lighter-skinned Blacks benefitted from favouritism. This may have been particularly true in the earlier days of the Home, when segregation, overt racism, and discriminatory practices were very much entrenched in society. Garnet believes that by the time residents came through in the 1980s, some things may have changed.

However, occurrences of favouritism based on skin colour were certainly apparent during his time there.

The staff's anger, abuse, and personal problems also affected their interactions with the children in the Home, and they would often take out their issues on the unassuming children. Garnet remembers one staff member who used to come through the dorms in the middle of the night to do checks. Without warning, she would come in with a skinny switch that stung and begin beating the children out of their sleep. The children didn't know what they were being punished for. And with no protection from the short potato sacks they wore for bedclothes, the switch was guaranteed to leave welt marks across their legs and body.

For Garnet, the Home was a prison. "It was like going through the gates of hell," he says. "How could we have a peaceful sleep?" For Garnet and others, there seemed to be no contentment during the day, and no guarantee of rest during the night.

Garnet was aware that other children his age who lived outside of the Home had a freedom to come and go that he did not. "I felt like other young people were out learning about life, making mistakes, going to movies, and having fun at dances. But we were in the Home, trapped. I was sixteen before I was even allowed to go anywhere alone. I didn't know anything." By the time Garnet met his first girlfriend, he knew absolutely nothing about dating. Even when his mother visited him at the Home on a few rare occasions, there was always a matron standing nearby the entire time ensuring he didn't say anything he wasn't supposed to.

Garnet says he never saw a doctor once throughout his thirteen years at the home. A medical professional would have noticed some of his bruises and injuries. Perhaps he would have felt safe enough to tell a doctor what was happening to him. But he never had the opportunity. Garnet had a cyst on his body for years and the Home would not take him to have it treated. Instead, they put oatmeal plaster on it—some sort of home remedy. "By the time I was sixteen, I had pyorrhea of the gums," he says, describing an advanced-stage gum disease that led to him having all his teeth removed when he was nineteen.

Throughout his time at the Home, Garnet does not remember owning a toothbrush—all the boys had to share one. Brushing was just one quick swipe and then on to the next child. And everyone had to wash their hands in the same water, in a basin by the door. At bath time, the tub was filled once. "Each child took a turn bathing in the same water. If you were first, you got the fresh bathwater. If you were near the end, you got to bathe in the dirty water that over fifteen others before you had just bathed in." Garnet thought that all of these practices were a normal part of growing up.

Garnet now feels empathy for his mother. As an adult, he doesn't blame her for the circumstances that led him and his brothers and sister to the Home. She was alone, and people in the community watched her struggle but didn't help. There is anger among Garnet's siblings, which is natural given what they have been through. Some have dealt with their pain in destructive ways, burying it in alcoholism and promiscuity. They also suffer from depression. This is all too true for many other former residents.

In the 1990s Garnet's brother Peter was one of the first former residents to want to come forward and share his story publicly.

He contacted many others, hoping to form a united circle of support. If they all told their stories together, they reasoned, they would have a better chance of being believed. But at that time, many were not ready to come forward. Some were still in the midst of their pain, while others were too angry to relive it. Still others did not want to cause trouble within the community.

I spent hours with Garnet, just sifting through the many preserved binders, filled with articles, papers, and photographs—including the vast collection passed on to him from his brother Peter. Over homemade turkey soup and apple crisp, we unpacked a past that had been neatly stored away. As we emptied out the contents of his childhood baggage, the depth of his character became more and more obvious. The sum of the neatly collected documents represented the "lemons" that life had handed to him. The man he is today is a result of the "lemonade" he made with them. The lemons are still there, but instead of letting them sour his life, he has managed to use them to form the basis of the work he enjoys today.

At one point in Garnet's life, he promised himself he would never "do nothing for nothing" because of the way he was treated as a child. He also said he would never work with children. But for the last twenty-five years, Garnet has been doing exactly that: Never asking for anything in return, he shares the gift of his life experiences. He tells his story to teens, leaving a lasting impression on them. One principal told him that several youth from a school Garnet spoke to furthered their education after hearing Garnet's story and his words of encouragement. Three are studying to be paramedics, three have set their sights on law school, and two are studying to be doctors—all professions that should have been able to help Garnet and other residents when they were children. Perhaps these students' goals are their way of saying,

Just a few of Garnet's vast collection of awards and certificates for his work in the community.

"We heard you, Garnet." Regardless of their motivations for striving higher, Garnet's speeches have clearly had an impact.

Garnet has received dozens of awards for his outstanding community service, for his his impact on youth in schools, and for his selfless volunteerism. Certificates from government, community organizations, and schools alike cover the walls of his home and fill his neatly stacked binders. Numerous articles about him all have a place in his extensive collection. These accolades make up a significant and deeply satisfying part of Garnet's life. At Highfield Junior High, the school where he has spent his time for so many years, the students adore him. His decades of service as a volunteer and mentor have made him a permanent and welcoming fixture in the building.

Garnet credits his faith in God with helping him to turn the bad into good. The man he is now may well be the person he was always meant to be; growing up, he just wasn't in an environment that nurtured or celebrated his gifts. But by surrounding himself with a loving wife, son, and positive people, he was able to see in himself what had been hidden there all along. He never writes his speeches down, he just speaks from the heart. His heart is big and he has found plenty of room in it to share with others, even though no one shared theirs with him as a child. He hopes that by continuing to convey his wisdom and experiences, he can encourage others to set high goals for their lives and not let anything stop them from realizing their dreams. I can sense Garnet's awareness of the impact he is having on young people. I knew for certain by the end of my visit that he has found his calling.

Below is a poem written by Garnet about living at the Nova Scotia Home for Colored Children.

Were You There?

Were you there when our dad stood in the yard while we were pushed into the car?

Were you there when they took us to the poorhouse, also considered the crazy house?

Were you there when we arrived and did not know anybody in that strange place?

Were you there when we were separated from our brothers and were not told we had a sister there?

Were you there when we were outside in the cold during winter for hours until it was time for lunch or dinner?

Were you there when we were hungry and cold and could not ask for food?

Were you there when we had to eat food from the pig farm and then hide it in the woods for later when we got hungry?

Were you there when we got a beating for nothing?

Were you there when we were sleeping at night and we woke up to someone beating us for something we had done during the day?

Were you there when we had to work on the farm picking potatoes and peas and got a beating if we were caught eating?

Were you there when they took all the candy and clothing away our mother had brought for us?

Were you there when the farmhand took us down to the basement and beat us while the help watched?

Were you there when we were sick and never got to see a doctor or dentist?

Were you there when I had my teeth removed because of gum disease?

Were you there when I left the Home with no education?

I didn't know how to read or write or do math.

I could not get a job.

The worst thing for me was going through life without an education.

Were you there? No!

Chapter 6

Starann

I was just nine years old when me and my siblings were taken from our mother and placed in the Home. That was in the mid-seventies. I was the oldest of three. The others were five and seven and I was their protector. I cared for them and looked out for them, kind of like a mother figure. Our mother was there, but she had her own issues. I believe both of our parents loved us, but they weren't able to be there for us the way that we needed it. Eventually, my mother had a breakdown and was admitted to a mental hospital for treatment. I remember a social worker coming to our house. My mother was home at the time and she spoke with the social worker. It seemed like everything was fine and the social worker left. But at a later date, the social worker came back again. This time, our mother was not at home. I was there, caring for the younger ones. The social worker told me that she was taking us all for a drive to get a treat, so of course we agreed to go.

As an adult reflecting on her childhood, Starann is full of fight. She has an aura of persistence and determination. Her resolve, despite many defeats in a tiring battle, appears almost as a mechanism of

Starann, left, sits with her siblings just before they are sent to the Home. Deanna, far right, lost her battle with cancer in March 2015.

her desperate fight for survival, rather than a choice. All of her life, she says, she's had to stay hyper-alert, never allowing her soul to rest. There has always been an element of danger. That same element—not the physical danger, but the memory of it—was alive and immediate during her interview.

"The social worker lied. We weren't going for a treat at all," she says.

And there would be no treats for Starann. The next thing she remembers is the drive up the long gravel road that led to the tall, three-storey building. The social worker never explained why they were being placed in the Home, nor how long they would be there. There was no word about whether they would ever see their mother again, says Starann. The trauma of being taken from her mother and sent to this strange place caused Starann incredible stress.

It was like I walked around blank for the first year, just trying to understand the things I was seeing and the way I was being treated. I remember being made to fight the other children. One of the girls was my best friend. She was always being forced by staff to beat up others, so she was seen as a bully. I don't believe my friend wanted to fight but she really didn't have a say. It was either fight or be beaten. And even though we were friends, we were made to fight each other too.

Many other former residents also reported that when you were put on the spot to fight, a friend or even a sibling could have been standing across from you. Sometimes children would get beat up so badly they would collapse. They were simply left there. No help, no doctor, no comfort.

"I used to pick fights with the girls I shared a room with. That was so that I could get moved to a different room," Starann remembers. "People saw me as a troublemaker, but it worked, and I got moved. I thought it would be better in the new room, but it was worse. That's when the night visits started."

Starann was now alone in a room, separated from the other girls. Easy prey for male staff, she was approached with anything but good intentions. She vividly recalls the first time a male staff member entered her room. She could feel him walk closer to her bed. Without warning, he began to molest her. She was so afraid and shocked. The staff member told her not to say anything, and that no one would believe her. She had already been in trouble on multiple occasions for acting out and causing fights, so to Starnn, those words rang true. She kept silent.

Starann's siblings were also not immune to the staff's abuse. She was always checking on them and looking out for them, but was helpless in preventing their daily suffering.

I remember wandering up the stairs one day to the boys' section. My brother hadn't come down with the other children so I wanted to make sure he was okay. When I burst into his room, I couldn't believe what I saw. My brother and another male resident were on their hands and knees on top of their beds. I saw two male staff having sex with them from behind. My brother and the other boy were crying their eyes out. One of the male staff noticed me and yelled at me to get out. I just shut the door.

Starann was devastated by what was happening to her brother. She could do nothing.

"On another occasion, my sister was being punished by a staff member," she recalls. "I don't remember what she did, but she was five…whatever she did annoyed the staff member and she beat my sister viciously." The incident happened in the little girls' dorm. Starann was on the other side of the door. She wasn't allowed to enter, but could hear her sister screaming for the beating to stop, and other children screaming in horror.

"I could hear my sister cry. Then the crying stopped," says Starann. "A little while later I watched that staff carry my unconscious sister out of the room. My sister's five-year-old body was very little at the time. She looked dead."

Starann had no idea where her sister was taken. "I did not know whether she was taken to *that* room on the third floor or whether she was dead." Children weren't allowed out of "that" room, and no other children were allowed in. No doctor was ever called to the Home. Starann thought her sister was dead. She approached the staff members daily for the next few weeks begging for news of her missing sister.

"They were cruel," she says. "One staff I asked in particular about where my sister was, said to me, 'Maybe she's dead, maybe she isn't.' I had to try and sleep each night wondering if my sister was alive and if I would ever see her again." Starann also had to continually deal with the sexual assault by male staff members.

Like so many others, Starann felt that no one loved or cared for her. But what was evident in her story and through her words was that she showed a solid love for her siblings, despite not being shown any by her caregivers. I understood it quickly. It permeated her speech. "I felt like it was my job to protect them," she said multiple times throughout our interview. Everything was for them: her defiance, her rebellion, and her need to protect.

Three weeks after the beating, Starann's sister appeared. "When I saw her I ran to her and hugged [her], and wanted to know where she was," she says, remembering that day. "She looked fine. Her injuries had healed. But while we were hugging, a staff member stood over top of us making sure she didn't tell me anything." For many years, Starann suffered from guilt about what happened to her siblings. She believed it was her responsibility to protect them and that she hadn't done enough. But as a child, she could never be held responsible for the actions and decisions of the adults whose job it was to protect them.

Starann (age eleven) and her sister Deanna (nine) in the Home.

Over the years, Starann's fear turned to anger and resentment. She became feisty, and staff called her a troublemaker. Once, she witnessed a female staff member pounding on a resident named Robyn with a bunch of keys in her hand. "She was on top of Robyn in the hallway punching her in the face. I saw blood on Robyn's face an on the floor all around her." Starann said she tried to help Robyn by pulling the staff off of her. In retaliation, the staff swung around and punched Starann in the mouth with the keys in her hand. Her mouth was full of blood. Someone called the police and when they arrived, they spoke with Starann. "I told them what happened and showed them my bloody mouth," she says. Starann stood there as the officer read her file. The staff member had called Starann's injury "self-inflicted."

"I do not believe that the police ever did anything as a result of the vicious assault to Robyn and myself," says Starann.

Starann's newly formed tough exterior helped her discover clever ways to ward off staff members' sexual advances. She recalled many times where she would fight back or threaten to tell someone. Sometimes that was enough to make her molester back off. Starann credits her survival instincts kicking in because she'd had to ward off sexual predators before. Both of Starann's parents were alcoholics and prior to the Home, she remembers her grandfather frequently stepped in to babysit her and her siblings. But he had ulterior motives.

Starann calls her strength "Survival Syndrome": she was constantly on high alert to protect herself. Those same instincts ultimately rose up and prevented her from being brutally raped while she was at the Home. Others were not so fortunate, and in some cases, those rapes resulted in pregnancy.

A former resident and a friend of Starann's was one of those young women. During the entire pregnancy, she was separated from the other children. Once she had her baby, Home staff took it from her. No one ever knew where the baby went or what became of him, until many years later, when the resident was able to track down her child, an adult by then. When they reunited, he revealed to his mother that during his search, he was told by the Home he was given away because his mother did not want him. Luckily, he learned the truth about his mother's story.

As tough as Starann was, some staff members continually tried to crush her spirits, often using harsh words. "Staff were constantly telling us kids that we were ugly, unwanted, stupid, and would never amount to anything," she remembers. "Girls were told they were only good for laying on their backs." Countless former residents have echoed Starann's words. Former resident Tracy Dorrington stated in her affidavit, "Staff members would regularly call us stupid, useless…and would often tell the girls that no man would want us."

Verbal abuse cuts deep and remains long after physical wounds have healed. After hearing such things repeatedly over many years, with nobody affirming the opposite, a child will most certainly believe them. Feelings of worthlessness, depression, anxiety, and hopelessness describe the childhoods of too many residents who passed through the Home.

One day, retaliating against such harsh mistreatment—and in particular, the staff member who had punched her in the face—Starann grabbed a large rock and threw it through that staff member's office window. As punishment, she was badly beaten with a hockey stick. When police arrived over the broken window and noticed her bruises, staff informed the officers that Starann often beat herself up for attention. Starann recalls going to a member of the board and telling them what happened. She was angry that staff reported the incident in her file as a self-inflicted injury. The board did nothing. At that point, Starann knew she had no voice, realizing just how far some Home staff would go to ensure the children remained silent, fell in line, and obeyed.

Starann wanted revenge. One day in protest, she and a few others broke into the office where the files were kept. "We pulled out all the files we could and set them on fire," she says. "We watched the files burn to ashes on the floor then we snuck back out of the office. When staff found out what happened, they were furious. I remember the staff lining all the kids up and asking us about what happened to the files and who broke into the office. No one would tell." In a show of solidarity, the children all claimed to have done it. It was an example of oppressed youth doing what little they could to speak out in a voiceless environment. Starann and the others were innocently unaware of the repercussions; however, they escaped punishment in that situation because the few who knew the truth kept their secret. Unfortunately, the valuable information contained in some of those files held the missing pieces that many former residents would later come back in search of. Now they will never get those answers.

For Starann, Christmas was not a season of festivity and glad tidings at the Home. She remembers staff members kept the gifts her parents left for her. What little she claims they received arrived in a garbage bag, which they took back to their rooms. She doesn't remember a traditional Christmas around a tree, opening gifts, or spending important time with fellow residents. As Christmas came around every year, she had nothing to look forward to. It was the same daily, for meals.

"It seemed like we barely got enough to eat," she says. "I didn't like to eat the food that was prepared by the cooks because in my mind, I felt like they were trying to poison us." Although Starann knew that wasn't the case, she couldn't be convinced otherwise. So she didn't eat a lot. She'd have things like milk and cereal, but avoided the cooked meals whenever she could. At times, during the colder months, the Home received deer meat and other wild game, but she tried to avoid it. They also received donated food from local stores. She wouldn't eat that either. No one seemed to notice her lack of appetite. If they did, no attempts were made to talk to her about it. Starann recalls an incident in which a staff member dropped that night's dinner on the floor. After watching as a staffer picked it up and dished it out to the residents, Starann told the others what she had seen and not to eat the meal. Staff were puzzled as to why the residents had no appetite that evening.

Ironically, the most devastating event of Starann's life at the Home happened while she was away from it.

"I had been begging to go visit with my relatives in Ontario for a long time," Starann explains, "but the answer from staff was always no. I was so desperate to go." When she was about thirteen, four years after first arriving, the Home began making arrangements to place Starann's siblings in a foster home. She had no idea. None of the staff informed the overprotective older sister that she was about to be separated from from her brother and sister, the two youngest. Instead, the staff agreed to let her go to Toronto to visit family. Starann was overjoyed. She was told it would be her reward for passing grade seven. While she was away, her younger brother and sister were shipped off to a foster home.

The foster parent, Jane Earle, would later tell me that she and her husband, Gordon, understood the children were not to be separated and were willing to take them all, but it was the Home that made the decision to allow only the younger ones to go. The two older sisters, Starann and Deanna, were left at the Home. Jane expected that once the younger ones got settled, the other two would be allowed to come.

When Starann returned to find two of her siblings gone, she was devastated. She had been promised she would not be separated from them. With no real explanation from the Home, the resulting trauma caused Starann to hate and resent the foster parents, believing they purposely separated her from her younger brother and sister. With no counselling or support from the Home or the child welfare agency who placed her there, Starann's feelings about this traumatic separation festered for years. She wouldn't learn the truth until adulthood.

As she got older and bolder, Starann made many attempts to run away from the Home. She would make her way back to Truro to her father, which was almost an hour away by car. Each time, she recalls, he had to make the heart-wrenching decision to send his daughter back.

I was taking off and running away almost every week. But because I was a ward of the Province, my father would explain that I couldn't stay and he would take me back to the Home. Eventually, that male staff [member] who was molesting me started coming to look for me. Every time he found me and brought me back, he would beat me up for running away. He never left a mark on my face, but my body was always full of bruises and possibly broken bones. I never got to see a doctor. And every time I would run away and he would find me, he would beat me up worse than the time before.

The same staff member has been named in numerous affidavits of former Home residents, including that of Harriet Johnson, alleging rape and sexual abuse.

When Starann returned to the Home, bruised and in pain, it would have been nearly impossible for staff not to notice that she was badly hurt. Nobody said anything. Nobody helped her. The social worker who'd initially dropped her off over five years prior was nowhere to be found. The one person responsible by law to protect Starann had failed her miserably.

Despite the horrors of her past experiences, Starann has since placed herself on a path to recovery. She was sixteen when she finally managed to run away from the Home for the last time. No one found her and she never looked back. She admits to being naïve when she got out into the world. At such a young age, she was inexperienced and didn't possess street smarts. She had only known the confines of the Home. And despite all she did to keep from being raped by staff there, her first terrifying experience on her own involved being raped by a stranger. It's an incident she is still, to this day, unable to speak about in detail.

Starann's ideas about relationships were also moulded by her life at the Home. She ended up in an abusive marriage that lasted a few decades. She has since spent a lot of time with counsellors in an effort to come to terms with what happened to her. She was able to leave her marriage and move forward after many years of abuse and is just now beginning to accept that what happened to her and to her siblings was not her fault. Starann feels that finally talking about her past has helped her to begin healing from it.

Many former residents are still not at a place where they are able talk openly about their experiences. Some are more than willing to share. Each one of them must come to terms in their own way and their own time. For Starann, it has been a long road. She remained connected to her siblings, though there was still a lot of pain among them. Added to that pain was the tragic 2015 passing of Starann's sister, Deanna Johnson Smith, a high-profile leader in the court battle against the Home. As private as she was, Deanna bravely stepped forward as one of the first plaintiffs in the class action suit against the Home and the Province. All the while, she was battling breast cancer. On March 21, 2015, Deanna Johnson Smith passed away, leaving behind two children and an incredible legacy of courage and strength in the face of her troubled past. Lawyer Ray Wagner credited her for being a significant contributor to the successful class action settlement. "She was always the solid rock," he told the *Globe and Mail* in an article about her passing.

Starann's post-traumatic stress disorder diagnosis is surely a common one among many of the Home's former residents who suffered similar abuses. Several others, including Robert Borden and Tony Smith, two of the first to file individual lawsuits against the province, have been diagnosed with PTSD, which became an important factor in their legal fight against the government.

Through journaling and by sharing her story, her truth, Starann has shown courage. And in speaking about it, her abusers no longer have power over her. As a child, she had done nothing wrong; she was a victim. Now she is a survivor.

Chapter 7

Richard

TODAY, RICHARD EXUDES A QUIETNESS of spirit, an air of contentment almost. It doesn't appear to come from the surface but deep inside of him.

It was 1964 when he arrived at the Nova Scotia Home for Colored Children. That year, and the years before and after, the Home staff saw a lot of children transferred into their care from Liverpool, on Nova Scotia's South Shore. Richard knew many from his community who were taken from their families and shipped to the Home. He was eight when he and his siblings were piled into a car for the long two-and-a-half-hour drive.

My siblings were twelve and fifteen. My parents couldn't take care of us. All they needed was some financial help and support from the government, but they didn't get it. Instead of helping them that way, they took us away from our home. If social workers would have just helped the families living in poverty instead of separating them, a lot of us would have been spared the pain.

The situation of many Black families in Liverpool and in other parts of Nova Scotia at that time was similar. Many were struggling financially, as it was difficult to find steady work. Parents did what they could to make ends meet. Government assistance, even unemployment assistance, was insufficient support.

Richard's first day at the Home was unusual.

"The moment we walked into the Home, we were stripped down naked and placed in a tub. They told us we needed to be washed in case we had lice. Then they dried us off and dosed us with talcum powder," he remembers.

He also recalls his experience with the social worker: "I remember it was a male social worker who dropped us off but we never saw him again until months later, when he showed up close to Christmas time. He dropped off a [Sears] Wishbook [and] let me pick something out of it. I didn't get to keep the toys and play with them when I wanted to. The staff would only let me play with them at certain times then they would take them back and put them away until the next time."

Richard remembers that any treats, fruit, or candies from visitors were immediately taken away by staff and never given back. Those recollections are in line with a 1966 report from one of the department's social workers, who visited the Home and documented that, with no more than a bed and a chair, its sleeping areas were inadequate and cramped together. "No toys, clothes, or pictures on the walls. No place to keep personal belongings could be seen."

Richard often wondered why his social worker never asked him if he was okay. When some staff members with darker skin called him names, like "pale-face," because his skin was very light, or he witnessed inappropriate things happening to other children, he had no one to tell. But Richard does remember one staff member who was different, and treated him very well. "She was good to the children," he recalls. "She always tried to do what she could to help us."

Richard has also kept a photo of himself with a few other residents who had an opportunity to leave the Home and attend the 1967 Expo in Montreal. It was a great escape; he got to spend that time away from the Home and forget about the pain of his life. He cherishes that memory fondly.

Unfortunately, that was not the norm, and the staff person Richard spoke of fondly couldn't be there twenty-four hours a day. She couldn't see or know everything. She was not able to prevent the severe physical punishment and cruel psychological mistreatment that Richard and his siblings suffered at the hands of the other staff members.

> *I used to get beatings a lot with a tennis racket by staff. I used to be afraid to go to school because I thought that the other children could somehow be able to tell that I was being beaten. Sometimes, I would hide on the roof of the small cottage beside the Home to avoid a beating, especially if I knew it was going to be a severe one. There was a staff [member] who used to stand at the door with the tennis racket waiting for the children to return from school. We were told each day to take our "good" clothes off after school and put the old ones on.*

Most households in the community operated that way in those days, not having laundry facilities. Some were on a well system so water couldn't be wasted. Having the children save their good clothes for school and play in their old ragged ones was quite normal. But being severely beaten with a tennis racket if they didn't get their clothes off right away was not normal. As psychology has taught us, placing unrealistic expectations on children can cause them to be unnecessarily fearful, to experience feelings of inadequacy, and/or believe that they can't do anything right. According to Binggeli (et al) in *Psychological Maltreatment of Children*, these rigid or unrealistic expectations placed on a child, especially when there is a threat of loss or danger if the child does not live up to them, is coined as "terrorizing," and is one of the six major types of psychological maltreatment. The way we view terms such as this with respect to children is being continually evaluated and evolved in an effort to fully understand what long-lasting effects they have on children into adulthood.

"And if one child did something wrong a lot of times everyone would get punished," says Richard, "especially if no one came forward to admit the wrong. I feel like most of the staff there just didn't have the specialized education needed to take care of the children."

Luckily, Richard was among the first waves of residents who got to attend school off the Home's property. Correspondence between the board and the department at the time shows that the Home was urged to allow some of the children to attend William Ross School, just down the street. The directive came after observational reports from a few of the department's workers that the children had nothing to do, very little extracurricular involvement, and no other relationships outside of the Home.

With constant beatings and psychological abuse, Richard lived in fear amongst the other children at school. "How could you concentrate when all you could think of was what was happening, or going to happen, when you got home?"

Richard was not sexually abused at the Home, but says he witnessed some disturbing things. "At night, female staff would walk around us boys with barely any clothes on," he admits. "We could see their private areas." The Nova Scotia Department of Justice defines sexual abuse as "the improper exposure of a child to sexual contact, activity, or behaviour." For instance, showing children pornographic images or forcing them to watch sex acts is catagorized as indecent exposure and therefore has the potential to cause harm. The Home's staff members were in positions of power; the boys were minors. Sexually arousing these young boys was inappropriate and constituted a form of sexual abuse.

"I do remember always hearing girls in their dorms crying through the night," Richard says. "We had an idea of what was happening to them, but we were helpless. We all knew they were being sexually abused by staff but we were not allowed to say anything about it." It would have been extremely difficult for a child to lie helpless in bed knowing another child was suffering nearby at the hands of an adult. The psychological implications of such trauma are certain to cause problems well into adulthood, as they did for Richard.

Before he was taken to the Home, Richard was already a victim of medical neglect. He recounted being a small child when he was hit by a train. He lives with a steel plate in his head as a result, and doesn't feel as though he received the ongoing medical treatment that he should have been getting at the Home. With all of the beatings, and even those times when he injured himself outside playing, he was never sent for medical treatment. He has only one recollection of a doctor's visit: "One night while I was asleep, some of the other boys were being mischievous. They tied a rope to a piece of steel, hung the rope, and let the steel drop. It fell on my head and split it wide open. Staff took me to the doctor. But that was the only time I ever remember going."

Like other residents, Richard says there was never enough to eat. Breakfast was a very small portion of cereal or oatmeal. Supper was the one full meal they did receive, but wasn't complete:

Us children would get the soup with no meat in it, and the staff would get the meat that should have been in our soup. We had to be outside all day until it was time to eat. Even on bitter-cold winter days, they wouldn't let us come in. We had to do what we could to stay warm until we were allowed back in. We never received snacks throughout the day, only the food that we ate together during our main meals. I would be so thirsty some days that me and the others would drink water from the puddles in the yard. A lot of times we snuck and ate the stuff in barrels that was brought from the bakery for the pigs. Whatever we could do to eat.

By age eleven, Richard was no longer able to endure the harsh treatment, and he ran away from the Home every chance he got.

I wasn't even a teenager yet when I started running away. I kept trying to make my way back to Liverpool. I got beaten severely when I was taken back. One day, me and one of my cousins from Liverpool made a plan to run away. He was living in the Home too. We got as far as Brooklyn, but we were hungry and tired, and we were lost. We didn't know at the time that we were only about five miles away from Liverpool. We knocked on a stranger's door hoping to get some help. The woman who answered the door was nice and she let us in. But she knew we were boys who had run away from the Home. She told us she heard it on the radio.

Police came and drove the boys back to the Home. Once again, Richard says he and his cousin were severely punished when they returned. But the beatings weren't enough to stop his attempts to escape. He was determined to be free of the Home.

Another time, Richard recalls that he and his cousin hitch-hiked: "A Black man picked us up. We told him our story and why we left. He seemed to already know about the Home and about how staff treated the kids. He took us as far as he was going and then he gave us some money to help us get the rest of the way to Liverpool. He said the money was to help us get away from that place."

Sadly, the attempt failed, and again they were found and returned.

Richard began his schooling at the Henry G. Bauld Center, on the Home's property, at age eight, and then continued on at William Ross School, just a short walk down the street. At thirteen, he was in the right place at the right time, and it saved his life: "I remember I was singing in a Christmas concert at William Ross School. After the concert, a couple approached me in a nearby classroom and asked if I would like to come and live with them in Lake Loon, which was only about five minutes away from the Home. They had already taken in one boy from the Home previously."

Richard was extremely excited; this was his chance at a normal life. The couple spoke to the Home and, in no time, plans were set for Richard's favourite staff person to drive him to his new home on Christmas Eve. But there was a huge snowstorm that day, and they could not pick him up.

Children walking back from William Ross School, located just down the street from the Home.

"I was so disappointed," he recalls. "I had all my hopes up and I didn't want to spend one more day in misery at the Home. But that staff person understood how badly I wanted to go and she ended up coming through for me." In a selfless act, she told Richard she would brace the storm and try to drive him to his new home. It took them a long time, but eventually they arrived safely.

That night, Richard slept in a comfortable bed. There were no beatings, no kids crying out in the night from assaults, no empty stomach. When he woke up that next morning, it was Christmas—a real Christmas. The tree was full of gifts. "I couldn't believe they had bought me just as many gifts as they did for the other kids who lived there," Richard recalls. The gesture made him feel important and special. It would be the first of many.

Eventually, a family in Dartmouth adopted one of Richard's sisters. His other sister, after running away from the Home several times, made her way back to Liverpool with a female cousin and was taken in by an aunt and uncle.

Richard was ill prepared for life when he finally left the Home. He didn't even know how to be close to another human. He said he didn't trust them. He wondered why they wanted to love him. As an adult, he took out his anger and feelings of low self-worth on those who tried to get close to him. Personal relationships failed because he was so damaged and was still carrying around his dreadful past. In his romantic relationships, he was the boss and his spouse had to listen. Domination, power, and control were the only methods he knew; they had dictated his relationships during his most impressionable years.

"With all the problems I had in relationships," says Richard, "I always wished those in charge of us at the Home would have just taught us some life skills and caring, how to treat people, and how to become good parents. Instead we learned not to trust people." Instead they learned anger and sadness. They learned to believe they were worthless.

Richard's wife is by his side as we talk. She is the pillar he has leaned on. And he does not neglect to identify her necessary role in his life, as a friend and his rock. "She is my biggest supporter," he says. I can sense that, after many disappointing and failed relationships, Richard feels blessed to have finally found someone who loves him in spite of his past. Perhaps she shares some responsibility for his newfound sense of peace. He suffered through a horrific childhood, and still I believe he managed to find a peaceful corner of his spirit where he found respite and stayed to benefit from all of its comfort.

Richard agrees that he has lived a very hard life, but he's continually working to remain focused on the positive. He survived it all despite the odds. He didn't get what he needed as a child, but he worked to get what he deserved as an adult: a loving family, a compassionate and understanding wife, support from his community in Liverpool, and, finally, acknowledgement from the government of Nova Scotia.

Although the government failed him and his siblings, the public apology was an immensely important step forward for Richard and the many former residents who waited so long for healing and closure. "Hearing the apology was good because for so long no one believed us," he says. Richard's tragic life is no longer a hidden secret. The wrongs done to him and to many others have been exposed, their stories revealed. Richard is a contented man because after all of those years, somebody finally believes him.

Chapter 8

Olive

ANGER, DEPRESSION, AND SADNESS FILLED the once-innocent life of Richard's older sister, Olive. She knew her mother loved her and her siblings but she had few resources and fewer choices. Their family lived in a three-room shack.

"We were taken from our mother for a short time early on, and then we were eventually placed back in her care," says Olive, now in her sixties. "But when we were taken from her for the final time and shipped to the Home, that was the last time I was back with her until I was an older teenager."

Olive's words come hurriedly as she speaks, rushing out in succession, and sometimes one on top of the other. There is a sense of urgency, as if the memories are so raw and disturbing that she has to release them right away, before the pain returns. She's a pleasant woman, though her frustration is evident. Her anger fresh and apparent. Her life was difficult, even before she went to the Home, as she recalls.

"In Liverpool, there were separations between the dark children and the light children," she says during our phone conversation. "I feel as if there was also discrimination from the social workers at Liverpool CAS [Children's Aid Society]. In my opinion, it was almost as if Liverpool Children's Aid was trying to get rid of all of [the community's] Black children." The sentiment was echoed by a former resident who wrote a blog post in response to a 2012 story posted on CBC's website:

I was a victim of this very place. There was no love no guidance they had no heart…For years and years I kept it all inside me too ashamed to say that I was even part of this awful orphanage. I had nightmares for years…it destroyed my family separating us as siblings. How could the children's aid break apart brothers and sisters because our skin was a different colour? Mom had some of us by a black father and the last three by a white man and they took us away from each other for life. I never ever got over that.

"A lot of the kids who got scooped up by Liverpool CAS were from poor families," Olive says. "They got dropped off at the Home and never returned to Liverpool unless they ran away. The social workers never checked on them and didn't even know whenever one of them left the Home. I remember a relative who had her children taken. There were eight of them. Five had a darker complexion and three were biracial. The darker ones were sent to the Home and the biracial children were placed somewhere in the U. S."

Whether the race issue was based in fact or feeling, other former residents who were also shipped from their communities in Liverpool and sent to the Home echoed similar sentiments.

In several documents and correspondence in 1966, between Alfred Kenney, the executive director of the Liverpool Children's Aid Society, and Fred MacKinnon, the deputy director of Child

Welfare, Mr. MacKinnon expressed deep concern over several issues, one being that the Liverpool agency was sending large numbers of Black children to the Home but did not provide supervision or follow-up visits to ensure the children were properly taken care of. MacKinnon referred to the Home as a "dumping ground" in one such piece of correspondence. Another of MacKinnon's concerns was that Mr. Kenney had no knowledge of when his wards left the Home, whether they were put into a foster placement, or where they were physically situated at any given time.

In a letter dated March 18, 1966, Mr. MacKinnon advised Mr. Kenney of a disturbing situation brought to his attention by the Home's board. The superintendent of the Home, Mr. Kinney, owned several houses that held foster parents as tenants. When staff arrived at foster placements to deliver government cheques for the wards, Mr. Kinney would be on hand to have the foster parents immediately endorse the cheques over to him for the rent they owed on his houses. In essence, as the Liverpool Children's Aid Society forwarded the wards' payments to the Home, they in turn provided cheques to the foster parents who had Liverpool wards in their care. Mr. Kinney was then recouping that money for himself, the documents said.

Other officials had concerns about the functioning of the Liverpool agency in Queens County. In a letter dated March 6, 1966, Supervisor of Corrections Tim Daley requested answers from Mr. Kenney to a series of questions, including the following:

- How many Queens County children are in the Home?
- When did you or your workers last see them in person to check on the care they are receiving?

- Have you ever collected progress reports from the Home regarding the children's school involvement?
- What supervisory services are you providing to the children while they are under the Home's care?
- Are the wards Liverpool placed in the Home still residing there, and if not, where they are located and what school are they attending?

In Mr. Kenney's response to the queries, he claimed that his office did not receive regular reports on the children, and went on to state that if a child had a particular need, the child met with him when he visited the Home. There is no indication of when or how often Mr. Kenny frequented the Home, or whether the children truly had an opportunity to address concerns to him.

———

Olive was close to fifteen on her first day at the home. She was so frightened by the atmosphere that she ran and hid under a table. She was quickly retrieved and, like her brother, Richard, has vivid memories of their arrival: "We were so humiliated," she remembers. "They had us standing there stripped naked in front of the other kids. They were strangers. We had to stand there while the staff cut me and my sister's hair off. Then they put us in a tub." A teenager at the time, Olive's body was developed. It was devastating for her to have her private parts so indecently exposed before a house full of children and adults she had never seen before. "There were other kids around. I was embarrassed," she says.

The Home's nursery, where toddlers were kept.

Olive also remembers being utterly heartbroken when she stumbled upon the Home's nursery one day. It was lined with cribs, wall to wall. Staff were responsible to tend to the babies, who were often ignored. She expressed empathy and, even then, could sense that these babies were desperately lacking love and attention.

I went in and saw the condition of the small toddlers that were kept in that middle dorm. The room was lined with playpens. The babies sat in their playpens for the whole day soaked with wet diapers. There was barely enough staff to care for them and you could smell urine and poop so strong coming from the room. I don't ever remember seeing the staff really interact with the babies. Those poor babies cried all the time and never came out of that room. One time I went in to pick up a baby because he was crying for a long time. A staff [member] came in and yelled at me and told me to get out of the room and mind my own business.

Olive also witnessed a lot of infighting among the residents. She was horrified to see the staff laughing as children got beaten to a pulp. And not only did she witness beatings by staff, she received many of them herself. The beatings had a deep psychological impact on her, she said. Olive tried to rationalize how the terror she was experiencing in at the Home was better than the care she received from her own home and community in Liverpool.

Like many other residents, Olive experienced extreme hunger and often stole food to survive. "There was always a lock on the sliding window that led to the kitchen. One day I figured out a way to break it, and I would climb in and sneak food," she says. "There was also a closet where staff kept treats and candy, like stuff that parents brought for their kids when they visited. I would break in there and sneak whatever I could get to eat." She also remembers stealing the day-old cakes off the back of the trucks that delivered them to the Home.

Olive thinks of her childhood as tragic. She lived an awful life, arriving at the Home during her vulnerable and sensitive teenaged years. She was robbed of an education and the chance to be a carefree teenager. Luckily, after living in the Home for about a year and a half, a family in Dartmouth adopted her in 1966.

Once she was out of the system, she made her way back to Liverpool. In order to begin healing and moving forward with her life, Olive recently sought the help of a psychiatrist. She still finds most of her past very difficult to talk about. Things happened to her that she has yet to come to terms with. She still suffers from flashbacks from the trauma and the hurt, but by taking steps forward one day at a time, she says, by talking with a counsellor and other survivors like her siblings, Olive is able to make it through.

Chapter 9

Lisa

LISA (NOT HER REAL NAME) became a resident at the Home in 1974. After spending about four years there, she was amongst the first group of children to be moved to the newly built facility. The new structure was still on Main Street in Dartmouth, adjacent to the Black community of Cherry Brook, and situated just a minute's drive down the street from the old location. But as was the case with many of the children from the Home, the now fifty-five-year-old's tragic childhood began long before she arrived there.

Lisa starts out strong as she shares her life with me. Her speech is deliberate and purposeful, while at the same time very relaxed. We share a level of comfort. We speak as if we have known each other for many years.

My mother is Caucasian and my father is Black. I was the middle child of three girls. Growing up, the neighbourhood we lived in [Sydney, Nova Scotia] was mainly white, and so were the surrounding communities. I didn't have a lot of interactions with Black people during that time but that soon changed.

The last day I would see my parents for many years was when I was four years old [1965]. My sisters were five years old and seventeen months. Our mother had abandoned us and she was nowhere to be found when a Children's Aid social worker showed up at the house one day. I'm sure someone must have called to report that she had left us in the house alone.

The social worker put the children in the car and pulled away. It was the last time Lisa would see her home. She remembers feeling as if something had broken inside of her. Her father would never be in a position to look for or retrieve his children. As they were driving away, Lisa saw him walking home from work, unaware that his children would be gone. It was at that moment the bond between Lisa and her mother was completely severed. For it her mother's actions, says Lisa, that changed the course of her life forever. Seven years would pass before Lisa, at age eleven, and her father would see each other again. And much longer before Lisa would be able to track down her mother for answers.

After she was abandoned, Lisa was shuffled through six different foster care placements. She says her spirit was already broken by the time she reached the Home at age thirteen. She was separated from her sisters. The youngest was placed in a Dartmouth foster home where she remained until adulthood, while her older sister drifted through the foster care system.

Lisa repeatedly felt the sting of rejection each time she was yanked from one home and placed into another. She had already internalized that she was unwanted and not good enough. What Lisa needed by the time she got to the Home, was a *home*. She had never experienced that. All she wanted was to have a family and feel wanted by them. She needed someone to care and understand what she had been through, someone to recognize the deep dark place she was in and appreciate the good things inside of her. Instead, she was rejected and sent away time and time again, as she bounced around foster homes with the reputation of being a bad kid. But she wasn't bad. She was a troubled child desperately crying out for love and attention and getting it however she could.

Negative behaviour always got the adults in Lisa's life to pay attention to her, so she continued to be purposely defiant. That craving also got her booted out of foster homes because nobody recognized her cries for help, she says. When she finally ended up in the Home, she'd already undergone five painful years in the system, mostly in white foster homes.

When I first got to the Home I experienced culture shock. Having very light skin and being raised in a white neighbourhood, I didn't have a lot of knowledge about Black people. All of my foster homes had been white families. Some of the homes had other foster children but they were also white. From what I knew and believed about Black people, they always stuck together as a community. But when I got placed in the Home and witnessed how some staff were treating the children, I was shocked. I kept asking myself how Black people could treat their own so horribly. I was even more shocked by the ones who weren't abusing the children. There were certain staff that always showed kindness and compassion. I'd always spoken highly of them for that. I even visited with them on a trip to Nova Scotia. But they and many others knew the children were being harmed but did nothing to protect them.

Even when they witnessed the abuse, staff remained silent, Lisa says. She said she couldn't understand why even those staff members who were relatives of some of the children didn't stand up and protect them. Most of the staff were friends with each other and some were related. No one wanted to tell on another, so everyone turned a blind eye. Because she was light skinned, Lisa says she also experienced racially insensitive and abusive comments from staff and some residents. She was continually harassed and picked on by those who accused her of not being Black enough.

"Certain staff would called us lighter-skinned children offensive names and would single us out," she remembers. They would smack her in the head as she walked by them or call her "albino" and "half-breed." Eventually, some of the other children mimicked the torment and picked on her as well. She suffered from tension headaches for years as a result.

"I was always being fed last by those same staff members," says Lisa. "They would give me food with very small portions and would make me wait until everyone got theirs before I could get mine. A lot of times they made me sit at the table where the smallest children sat and not with the children who were my age." Any opportunity she had, Lisa would hide food so she could eat later.

Lisa vividly remembers at one point being taken to the third floor, otherwise vacant, and locked up there alone. No one came to talk to her or explain anything. The floor was cold and eerily quiet. Lisa was not permitted to go downstairs or talk to anyone.They brought up hardly any food for her to eat and she was hungry. "The only time I got fed was at dinner and it was left outside the door," she says. She remained up there alone for a week and is still unsure why. "I cried every day and was so scared up there all alone and not knowing how long they were going to leave me."

And then there were the assaults. Lisa was always hyper alert, trying to avoid the male staff member who regularly molested her. She came to know the sound of her abuser's footsteps. "During bedtime routine, it seemed like I was always last to be allowed to take a shower," she explains. "And we were only allowed to shower once a week. Since I was last, I would often get trapped by that male staff [member] and sexually assaulted in the bathroom. After a while I started pushing a chair against the door so he couldn't come in while I was showering." Lisa also remembers rarely having clean clothes to wear in public. She recalls the humiliation of going to church and never having any clean underwear to put on. She didn't have many clothes and laundry was only done sporadically. So she often re-wore her dirty clothes many times over. For a body-conscious teenager, this would have been devastating.

Thankfully, while Lisa was living at the Home, the residents attended William Ross School with other children from the area. School was Lisa's escape. It was her only piece of normal. Her friends at school would often make negative remarks about their lives, or complain that they didn't have running water or a television. Lisa had all of those things but, in her words, they came with a price. She would have gladly taken the house with no television or running water in exchange for the Home with abusers and no love. School was the only place where Lisa could find peace, but each day it was only short-lived; she knew the horrors waiting for her when she got home.

———

Lisa's first sexual experiences were not consensual. A male staff member sexually abused her repeatedly. Memories of the abuse are still very painful for Lisa to discuss. As she tries to speak, she struggles. I can sense her trepidation. There comes a gasp, then tears. Those same tears that flow when she speaks about her mother. She fights for the words, but they won't come. They are blocked by the lump in her throat. She finally succumbs to the feelings and weeps. I sit in silence through those moments; her pain becomes my pain, and the silence is not only for her, it is for me as well. I begin to see, to hear, to feel all that she has been through, and it sweeps over me like a tidal wave.

In her own time and in her own way, Lisa brings herself back to the interview. I repeat comforting words of encouragement, reminding her of her great tenacity and strength. She continues on with her story. It is disturbing and unfathomable. She says she had already endured repeated sexual abuse in the Home with no one to turn to for help, but what she experienced as a preteen while a patient in a local hospital in the mid-1970s is an even darker episode in her young life.

I was out riding my bike one day and one of the male residents took it from me and took off down the driveway. I went running after him, yelling for him to give me my bike back. He eventually gave it back to me, but when I got back on it, he pushed me out into the road. A car was speeding up the highway and it struck and ran over me. They rushed me to the hospital. But while I laid in the hospital bed in pain, that same male staff [member] came to the hospital to visit me. When we were alone in the room, he reached his hands underneath the hospital blankets and started fondling me under the blankets. I couldn't believe that I was being sexually assaulted while I laid in a hospital bed, helpless. And that's what he did every time he came to the hospital. What kind of a person could do that?

In an unrelated event, Lisa was sent away for becoming pregnant while living at the Home. "I got pregnant [by] a boy in the community," she says. "The staff sent me to a home in Halifax for five months. When I had my baby, she was immediately taken away." Lisa's baby was born with spina bifida, a congenital defect that occurs during the first month of pregnancy when a baby's neural tube does not close completely; as a result, part of the spinal cord is exposed through the backbone. The baby was placed in the care of the same Children's Aid Society that was in charge of Lisa.

After the birth, Lisa was sent back to the Home. Her reception was painful. "The staff was cruel and belittled me in front of other residents, saying that I was a bad example," she remembers. "They called me names like 'red pig' and 'fat cow.' It was so humiliating."

Lisa was already emotional because she had just given birth, and to a baby with a serious medical condition. Lisa also took on the guilt of feeling as if she'd abandoned her child the same way her mother had abandoned her. In the short time she had with her in the hospital, Lisa spent every minute she could with her sick child. Before she left to return to the Home, Lisa wrote a letter to her infant daughter, telling her she was loved and explaining why her mother wouldn't be the person to raise her. When the Children's Aid worker came to take the baby, Lisa requested that the letter go with her and that if the baby lived to eighteen, she would receive the letter to read.

All the way back to the Home, Lisa cried, devestated. She felt a hole in her heart. No one helped her deal with the intense pain of giving up the child she had carried for nine months.

Finally I couldn't take it anymore. The constant name-calling from staff and the residents who mocked them. They had no right to judge me for having a baby when the things they were doing in that Home were disgusting. One day I was in the common room and a staff [member] kept making negative comments towards me in front of the other residents. She called me names and said that no one wanted me around. I got up from my chair and went downstairs, changed my clothes, and went to the corner store to hitchhike. I finally caught a ride into Dartmouth. No one followed me.

But Lisa had nowhere else to go.

Over the next while, still a ward of the Province, Lisa laid her head wherever she could—from couch to couch, in the hallways of buildings, and in the streets of Halifax. She grabbed odd jobs babysitting to make a few dollars. No one from the Home ever looked for her. Her Children's Aid social worker didn't inquire after her. For Lisa, it was further, painful confirmation that no one cared.

When she finally got her first place, it was in a rooming house with a bunch of strangers. She found herself hoarding food and hiding it for fear someone would take it. One girl who lived there harassed Lisa often, and she began to feel threatened and intimidated. She wondered if she would never escape.

It wasn't until she finally made her way out of Nova Scotia, as an adult, that Lisa was able to begin the long road towards healing. Though she says she is not there yet, Lisa is happy to be removed from the people and places that held her down for so long. "I realize that I am alone, but I am okay with being alone," she says. For her, writing has helped to express her thoughts and relieve the pain. It is a daily struggle.

Happily, a tremendous weight was lifted from Lisa when a social worker from Children's Aid came through for her by reuniting her with her child around 1997.

When my baby turned eighteen, CAS gave her the letter I had written all those years ago. Then one day I got a package in the mail from CAS. It was a collection of photos of my baby throughout her life and up to age eighteen sent by the foster parents. There was also a typed letter from my daughter who uses an assisted device because of her disability. She wanted to meet me. She also wanted me to come to her high school graduation. I made the trip back to Nova Scotia to meet my daughter and attend her graduation.

Lisa describes her daughter as a very sweet and loving girl whose foster parents did a wonderful job raising and loving her. The missing piece of the puzzle had been put in place. Lisa's daughter, now thirty, is doing well. Lisa maintains contact but is careful not to interfere with the life her daughter has with her foster parents.

Unfortunately, not all of the puzzle pieces would find their rightful place. Lisa felt that in order to truly move forward and put the past behind her, she needed to find and reconnect with her own parents. She needed questions answered. She eventually reunited with her father. She places no blame on him, and says she'll always cherish the time she got to spend with him before he died. Reconnecting with her mother, on the other hand, was neither as smooth nor easy. After much searching, Lisa managed to track her down in New Brunswick a few years ago.

My mother had been living in Sudbury. I wanted us to talk. I knew right away that there was no connection between us. I didn't get any warm vibes from the woman who gave birth to me. It seemed like our conversation was unproductive, because she refused to take responsibility for anything that happened. She was in denial about a lot of things. She told me that the only reason she had her daughters was because she wanted to have our father's Black babies. While my parents were dating, grandfather kept telling my mother not to keep seeing this Black man. Back then, it was looked down on for races to mix and make children. When the visit was over, I drove the long ride to take my mother home. When we got near her place, she asked me to drop her off at the corner so she could walk. She didn't want her new family to see her with me. She didn't want them to know she'd had three Black children from her past.

Once again, Lisa found she had been rejected by the woman who should have loved her the most. Lisa believes her abandonment and subsequent rejection by her mother is the root of the aching in her soul. Lisa expressed that she is hurt most because her mother never came back to get them.

Although her mother may never see it, Lisa wrote a powerful letter, in the form of a poem, addressed to her. Lisa's pain was on the surface as she read her poem aloud. She spilled the words that represented a culmination of all of her experiences. Her voice permeated my ears, her poetry slicing like a double-edged knife. Any mother's heart would have bled during those moments. As Lisa read her poem, I understood every thought she must have felt as she put pen to paper; the tears that must have fallen over the ink. Her gift for poetry was never nurtured or encouraged, and yet it managed to thrive. Her circumstances fuelled that gift.

Lisa journals regularly and documents her feelings. Still, she says she often finds it very difficult to trust and to get close to people. There have been many failed attempts to be close to her family, but these ties, she believes, have already been too severely broken. Her daughter is her only true connection: Lisa had four subsequent miscarriages in the years following her exit from the Home. Her last baby is buried in Barbados, where she was vacationing when her most recent miscarriage occurred.

Lisa she continues to reflect on each of the tragic events that brought her to where she is now. She is content in her environment but says that she is still haunted by the past. Lisa feels that it is her mother who set the wheels in motion when she made that fateful decision to leave her children alone that day. But one of Lisa's most powerful weapons, her gift of writing, has become a therapeutic outlet. I believe it is the vessel that will help carry her to the brighter side of her journey. She's not there yet—not even close. But her gift is leading her in the right direction.

Chapter 10

Other Stories

WHILE SOME OF THE MANY horrific tragedies to occur at the Nova Scotia Home for Colored Children have become prominent stories, repeatedly reported on, five in particular emerged during my research that I felt needed a voice.

The first story involves the experience of a woman who was raped at age fourteen. She had initially declined to be a part of the class action lawsuit, preferring to maintain her anonymity and privacy, but has since changed her mind. Reports show that as a teen, she was violently raped at the Home by a male staff member in 1983. The rape was reported to the Home's supervisor, who claimed to have conducted a thorough investigation. A major incident report was prepared and forwarded to the Home's board, which suspended the male staff member. As for notifying police to lay charges, the board decided to "shelve" the idea, pending further investigation. The victim received eighteen stitches as a result of the rape. Police were never notified, records show.

The second story centres on a special needs child living in the Home between the late 1970s and early '80s. His name was David Teed. Former residents describe him as a severely mentally handicapped person who had difficulty communicating. They recounted bearing witness to David's humiliation and abuse by staff. "I got along well with David and tried to treat him well. Staff treated David like an animal," says Harriet Johnson. In her sworn affidavit filed to the courts, Harriet states that she personally walked in on incidents where David was being sexually abused by the Home's male staff. Following the abuse, David would walk around rubbing his anus area, saying to no one in particular, "You hurt me," and "I'm gonna tell." Johnson's memories of the abuse were so vivid that she could still describe the pants David was wearing during one of the sexual assaults.

Harriet Johnson is not the only resident to have witnessed David's abuse. Others subsequently came forward to admit what they'd seen. But former residents and others concerned about his welfare ultimately lost contact with David over the years. Jane Earle, who served as the Home's executive director in 1980, recalls the last information she had on David's whereabouts found he had been moved to a group home outside of the city. The class action lawyers were unable to track him down for the purposes of the lawsuit. Today, David currently resides near Oxford, Nova Scotia. In 2002 he participated in the Special Olympics, where he excelled in soccer. He has since lived in various residential homes in that area. It is not clear whether he has any recollections of his treatment at the Home.

Calvin Paris, the subject of the third story, was another mentally and physically challenged former resident. He was at the Home when Jane Earle served as executive director. "Based on all the stories I have heard, from approximately fifty former residents, I would guess they [David and Calvin] were equally abused," she says. David's name appears often (as "David T") in statements made during media interviews with former residents, but Calvin Paris's name is rarely mentioned. Jane recalls incidents while executive director when she questioned staff about Calvin. Regretably, she says she wasn't then aware that most of the staff were complicit in the abuse of the children and that they were not coming forward with incidents that deserved investigation.

"I saw Calvin crying one day when I was walking through the building and I asked a staff [member] what had happened to him," she recalls. "She told me the kids were teasing him." Calvin didn't confirm or deny what the staff member had said.

Jane recalls a recent encounter with Calvin.

Calvin lives in Truro under deplorable conditions. I saw when I visited him at his place. Social Services admitted to me when I called that they weren't providing him with any services. He should have had home care and someone to monitor how he was living, from my perspective. His place was filthy, with old food lying around…. He called me to ask me to come and see him but when I arrived, he told me he couldn't remember anything about the Home. I have learned that he has had constant problems with the criminal justice system and it is suspected that this all stems [from] past sexual assault.

Not only does Calvin's current state demonstrate the far-reaching and deep effects of abuse, but it is also striking testament to the embarrassment we, as a society, should feel at how we care for our most vulnerable members. The hope is that Calvin has since received the help and support he so deserves, that services have been adequately put in place, and that he is surrounded by people who have his best interests in mind. "I plan to continue checking in on Calvin to see that the system gives him some proper help," says Jane.

The fourth is the tragic story of the late Anthony Langford, who had a hole in his heart. His fatal tragedy prompted Tony Smith, one of the first former residents to come forward with his story of abuse, and who has been a key driver in the many lawsuits against the Home, to begin his fight for truth and justice in the 1990s. Anthony was nine years old when he died under mysterious circumstances at the Home in 1969. Though this has never been definitively proven, several former residents have since come forward to say they believe Anthony was beaten to death by other male residents.

According to Tony Smith's account from the *Chronicle-Herald*, his friend Anthony was taken to hospital after that brutal beating. Within days, he was dead. Tony remembers Anthony was beaten very badly. He told *Herald* reporter Lousie Surette, "All of a sudden, my friend stopped crying and he slumped over with a funny colour to him." Anthony was taken to the hospital, where he died. Tony and the others who witnessed the beating were warned by staff not to tell anyone what they saw or they, too, would be beaten. A former resident named Peter (not his real name, according to the same reporter), also present when Anthony was attacked, corroborated Tony's account. He remembers Anthony as a frail and sick kid, and told Surette that he saw Anthony collapse that day.

Anthony's mother, Beverly Langford, tried for years to learn the truth about her son's death but continuously ran into brick walls. Staff members wouldn't talk. Around 1998 the RCMP confirmed they were looking into a complaint filed by Anthony's brother, Dennis, asking them to look into the facts surrounding his brother's mysterious death. He told news reporters from the *Herald* that he and his mother just wanted to know what happened. Those answers never came. RCMP said they had been told Anthony died during surgery and, as a result, had decided not to investigate. Beverly Langford passed away in the summer of 2005. Many unanswered questions went with her to the grave.

Today, Anthony Langford's tragedy lives on in his frustrated siblings. "When we were taken to the Home, my brother was just turning seven. I was eight. Who would have known that less than two years later my brother would be gone? To this day, my family still doesn't know the reason why," says his sister Stephanie from her home in Halifax.

Various stories have circulated over the years: Some say Anthony was beaten by older boys whom staff forced to fight. Others say his death was a result of repeated beatings by staff and older residents. And there are those who say he was attacked by a few of the boys who felt that Anthony was the cook's favourite.

Stephanie was outside in the field the day her brother was beaten but was told by another child who witnessed it that a few boys were upset because the cook had given Anthony an extra piece of cake. When Anthony walked into the playroom carrying the cake, a few boys began calling him names and throwing things at him. It escalated into a beating. No staff intervened.

"I had no idea my brother was even taken to the hospital," says Stephanie. "No one came and told me and my other siblings. It wasn't until after he died that a staff member told us he passed away. No one explained anything to us."

Stephanie will never forget the day of her brother's funeral. She and her siblings were told they could go. She recalls they made the long trek to the funeral location, a Baptist church in Lucasville, escorted by a male staff member. "When we pulled up to the funeral home, sometime after two o'clock, the place was empty," she says, her voice filled with frustration and disappointment. "The male staff told us that he must have had the times mixed up. The funeral had been at one o'clock. He told us before we left the Home that it was not until two. We missed my brother's funeral."

Stephanie and her siblings not only missed their final chance to see their brother since his death, but they would learn in adulthood, through conversations with their mother, Beverly, that the Home staff did not want their parents around. Stephanie's mother said staff assured her she would have her children together with her at Anthony's funeral, a time she would need them; she wanted to provide her children with the solace they desperately required. "My mother was clear. She specifically told them the time and location of the funeral," says Stephanie, becoming increasingly upset. It was still upsetting to her to learn as an adult how devastated her mother was when her children were not sitting beside her at the funeral to mourn together as a family. "They promised her we would be there. They lied to her. They didn't want us anywhere near our parents.

I believe they drove us late on purpose so that we would miss the funeral and not get to see our parents."

Anthony's remains were laid to rest in Lucasville, Nova Scotia. And to this day, his family has never seen a death certificate or any medical proof of his cause of death.

Stephanie had no idea that the last time she would see her brother would be the morning of his fatal beating. None of the boys who, she was told, attacked her brother, have ever approached her or her family to explain what happened, admit what they did, or to say they were sorry. She does know that one of them spent most of his life in and out of jail. She used to know the whereabouts of one of the others, but has not seen or heard of him in years.

Anthony's family feels the burden of guilt. "For years my mother blamed herself," says Stephanie. "She never came to terms with Anthony's death. She always blamed herself for not being there."

As Stephanie and her family laid Beverly Langford to rest in 2005, their sadness was heightened in knowing that their mother never found out what happened to her son. She took all that guilt to the grave, says Stephanie. In life, Anthony Langford never got a chance. In death, he never received justice. His family never received closure.

"Nobody was ever held responsible," Stephanie says. "And with the class action settlement, only the living receive compensation. But what about my brother? He died while he was in their care. What about what they did to my family? Everyone else received compensation. Shouldn't my family receive additional compensation for his death? Where is the acknowledgement for him and for what he suffered?"

During the Nova Scotia government's pending restorative inquiry, which will allow former residents the opportunity to publicly share their experiences, Stephanie plans to speak on behalf of Anthony, whose voice has been silenced.

———

The fifth story is about June Elwin, a Liverpool resident placed in the Home in 1940, along with her twin sister and an older sister and brother. She arrived as a toddler and remained there until she was thirteen. June told the *Chronicle-Herald* in a 2012 interview that a female staff member used to molest her and other girls in the Home. In court documents, she said the staff member would order June into her bedroom. When the staff woman came in, she would shut the door, grab June, and rub her body sexually against the young girl. Then she would force June onto the bed and climb on top of her. She would kiss her and fondle her breasts. June also said that there was a young child, only three years old, who would always be taken from her bed in the night by that same staff member. When she woke the next day to find the child's bed empty, June and the other girls would knock on the staffer's door pretending to want to say good morning, just to see if they could tell what was going on inside. But they already knew.

June Elwin also reported vicious beatings. She recalls one staff member in particular who would get the farmhand to retrieve his horse harness. That staff member would then make the child strip down then tie him to a post and watch as the farmhand whipped the boy or girl senseless. June witnessed a beating one time through a bathroom stall: when the boy was untied afterwards, he dropped to the concrete floor.

June, like many others, remembers always being hungry. "My constant hunger led to my stealing food that was intended for the garbage. I ate the garbage to compensate for the malnutrition I endured at the Nova Scotia Home for Colored Children," she stated in her affidavit to the courts.

June has fared much better after leaving the Home and the province. She remains vocal about sharing her childhood experiences. As a biracial woman, she experienced a lot of racism when she lived in Nova Scotia, and she told a reporter that once she was on her feet she wanted to leave the country for good because of the prejudice. Although all of June's abusers who worked at the Home have since died and will never be brought to justice, she continues to speak out and support the others who continue in their fight.

Chapter 11

The Social Workers

A History of Social Work in Nova Scotia

IN 2011 THE NOVA SCOTIA Association of Social Workers (NSASW) produced a document outlining its history. The document asserts that the catalyst for the growth of the social work profession in Nova Scotia was "crisis and chaos," in reference to the 1917 Halifax Explosion, which saw over one thousand children in desperate need of care due to parental death and loss of homes. Although the Canadian Association of Social Workers (CASW) was formed in 1926, at a time when there were few professionally trained social workers in Nova Scotia, it wasn't until 1931 that a provincial branch was formed in Halifax. It lasted only four years before being re-established in 1944. Gains throughout the 1930s, therefore, were slow. By 1939 the province had fourteen children's aid societies and only five professionally trained social workers, one of whom was Fred MacKinnon, the same director of Child Welfare who subsequently denied many of the Home's requests for adequate funding.

The birth of the Nova Scotia branch, a body formed with the help of the CASW to oversee regulation of social work in the Province of Nova Scotia, remains one of the profession's greatest accomplishments in this region. The first committee members, who had strong connections to the Halifax-based Maritime School of Social Work, saw the successful amalgamation of the school with Dalhousie University. The 1969 decision to unite the two was regarded as the solution to eliminating the problem of accreditation and other barriers faced by the school. Throughout the 1970s, the association experienced many bumps in the road to establishing regulations for social workers.

Membership and retention were ongoing struggles. Social workers began losing interest in the association's work. Many eligible members didn't feel membership was worth the necessary fees. There was also debate about whether allowing social workers with field experience but without academic training would lower the standards of practice for the profession. While dealing with these types of issues, the association was advocating for social justice and showing involvement in matters related to poverty, housing, and social welfare. Still, its greatest challenge lay in the discontent of its members and the issues of voluntary versus mandatory licensing and registration.

Small but important gains were made in the field in the 1980s. The debate about mandatory licensure versus voluntary registration was underway during this time. But the Department of Social Services supported a change that saw the term "caseworker" switch to "social worker" in civil service pay scales. This eliminated the long-standing concern over the professions being unrecognized and of unqualified workers being hired to fill roles that required professionally trained social workers.

Including "social worker" in civil service pay scales helped to ensure the most qualified applicants would be hired to fill those positions.

The association also took a strong public stance, via press release, against the minister of Community Service's exclusion of male-headed single families from the Family Benefits/welfare entitlement. Additionally, it arranged to have the deputy minister speak to its membership about the changes the government had made to the benefits provided to seniors, the disabled, and single mothers. The lack of progress made by government over the previous few years became a priority for the profession, as those who depended on government for income assistance continued to be marginalized and to suffer from inadequate housing and nutrition. The association's social action committee conducted a study to determine how the inadequate resources affected single mothers. Social workers also took the government, its task force on AIDS, and the human rights commission to task, seeking better protection from discrimination on the basis of sexual orientation.

The 1980s also saw the re-emergence of the Association of Black Social Workers (ABSW) following eight years of inactivity. Its resurgence met with concern from those in the field who felt that these special-interest groups would create division within the social work community. In her address to the association in 1988, Dr. Wanda Thomas Bernard emphasized that the mandate of the ABSW is to address issues of specific concern to the Black community. She further suggested that social work education is not culturally relevant for Blacks and that the Black community underutilizes services and supports in the community.

The great accomplishment for the profession, provincially, in the 1990s was the passing of the mandatory licensure legislation through the Nova Scotia House of Assembly. This legislature meant that in order to practice social work or use the title of "social worker," one had to, among other things, be trained, complete a designated number of social work hours (as a candidate for registration) under a practising social worker, and maintain professional development hours.

By the end of the 1990s, social workers were taking more interest in professional development, licensure, and membership. However, along with the gains came the headaches, such as the huge issue of reviewing and processing applications, and the issue of the grandparenting clause, which allowed applicants without social work training but who had worked in the field for a significant period of time to become licensed workers. The 1996 Board of Examiners report paints a picture of an overwhelmed regulatory body: In 1995 it had received 799 applications by deadline under the grandparenting clause. By the 1996 AGM, the board had reviewed 754. Out of those reviewed, 538 were denied registration because they did not meet the criteria under section 23 of the Social Workers Act (1993). Of those rejected, 238 applied for a review hearing. Of those applicants, the board managed to process 82 of those requests by 1996. The Board of Examiners consisted of nine volunteers who often had to schedule hearings on weekends to accommodate the workload.

By the year 2000, the association saw a 134 per cent increase in registered social workers. One of the highlights of this time is the revamping of the Code of Ethics of the Canadian Association of Social Workers, which affects the standards of practice for provincial social work associations across Canada, with a renewed push to improve social work practice.

Social Workers and the Nova Scotia Home for Colored Children

Child protection workers are considered agents of the government. They are mandated to serve the best interests of the child by investigating and acting on allegations of abuse. The Province (or State) grants a social worker the power to take whatever action is necessary to protect children from harm in accordance with the act that governs their jurisdiction—in the case of the Nova Scotia Home for Colored Children, this was the Children and Family Services Act. In many cases, child protection social workers have more power than the police, which is why their job must not be taken lightly. In Nova Scotia, for example, the police do not have the authority to remove a child from the home; if the situation is grave, they must contact child protection (or if afterhours, the emergency on-call worker) and the social worker, who is highly trained in the physical, emotional, and environmental needs of a child being removed from their family, will arrive on the scene to collect that child.

I have been in this position many times as a child protection social worker in Nova Scotia as well as in Ontario. I know firsthand what goes into this highly stressful role. Because of my work in the field, I was profoundly moved and genuinely interested in the role of social workers at the Nova Scotia Home for Colored Children, some of whom I've profiled in this chapter.

Jane Earle

Jane Earle is a long-time registered social worker with the Province of Nova Scotia and has worked in her profession for decades. She first had contact with the Home in the 1960s, when she did a placement with the Province while training under the Maritime School of Social Work. At that time, Jane was carrying a caseload of ninety-nine kids, which, by today's standards, equates to tragedies waiting to happen. One person alone cannot possibly manage this many children and families in need of services, placements, and solutions to immediate crises. To put this in context, there are now standards for how many cases a worker can carry: the number of cases social workers handled at that time is almost five times the current standard.

One of Jane's first assignments was to place three children in the Home. These children ranged in age from three to six, and were members of a very prominent, well-known family. Upon arriving at the Home, Jane met with its director, Mary Paris. She told Ms. Paris everything she knew about the children and that they were available for adoption. But both women knew adoption was most likely not going to happen. In those days, Black children didn't get adopted unless a relative came through. It was very rare that a white family would seek to adopt a Black child.

"When I first began dealing with the Home, I remember feeling like it was a very well-oiled machine," Jane explains in our interview. "The place looked spotless, and people looked content and happy. From the outside, everything appeared to be fine and I felt comfortable leaving the three children there." Though she didn't realize it, Jane's view of the home was misguided.

While I was director, I only worked during the days because I had the children at home. But I always smelled food cooking when I was leaving for the day. In my mind, I left thinking the children were about to receive a delicious, home-cooked meal. It wasn't until I talked to former residents years later that I learned they weren't

getting the food, and that only certain children got a full plate of
food while the rest barely received enough to fill their stomachs.

Jane Earle's recollections line up with observations and reports
filed by Community Services officials dating as far back as the
1940s. Those official documents noted that the Home staff appeared to help themselves to the hearty meals while the children
got almost nothing.

At this time, foster parents and other caregivers did not
transport children to appointments, as that was the responsibility
of the social worker. Through her involvement with those three
placements, Jane began to feel an attachment. "Working with
those three children led me to want to become a foster parent,"
she says. "I decided they would be the first children I would take
in. At first, I took short-term placements as requests came. By the
time I applied to get those three children in 1970, I was married,
had one other foster child, and one other child of my own."

Jane went on to accept a job at an organization for unwed
mothers called the Home of the Guardian Angel, but those three
children never left her mind. In her new job, Jane and two other
staff members each, at times, carried caseloads of up to fifty-five
women. The organization took in young pregnant girls from
outside of Halifax and all across Canada, who lived there for
the term and then gave up their babies for adoption before re-
turning home.

It was rare for me to see Black clients, because most Black families
back then let the girls keep their babies, or grandparents and other
family members took them and raised them. That stood out to me,
that sense of community and looking out for one another. I had

sympathy for the many young mothers who had no other alternative. Whenever I attended and spoke at conferences, like the ones hosted by the Black Baptist Women's Missionary Group, I always commended the community for holding on to their babies.

In the early 1970s Jane's husband, Gordon Earle, joined the Home's Board of Directors. She believed the board absolutely cared about the children. Other board members, like Brad Barton and Bob Butler, in Jane's opinion, all worked together to meet the needs of the children living there. However, a bone of contention for Jane was that when an issue was brought to the attention of its members, it usually died at the boardroom table. Attempts to address complaints often went nowhere because staff, for the most part, refused to talk or tell on each other, says Jane. She found this to be absolutely true when she accepted the position of executive director at the Home in 1980, one she held for ten months with no pay.

"Before I started in that role as ED, the Home was trying to begin a new venture," she explains. "They were going to use the cottage alongside the Home as a residence for a house mother." It was the same cottage that James Kinney, one of the Home's founders, and three generations of Kinneys called home. The cottage had several bedrooms upstairs and the idea was to foster a relationship between the house mother and Home staff so they could work together to support children with behavioural issues. Those children would then stay on at the cottage, receiving intervention from a trained worker.

"I applied for that position and was ready to move my family if I were chosen," Jane says. "I had the experience and a bachelor's degree. I was a long-time foster parent. But I was white.

I didn't get the job. It was between me and a Black staff member who had no formal training at all and didn't have the skills to deal with children facing behavioural challenges. She was given the job."

Even so, the idea of the cottage and house mother would never come to fruition. Jane continued to foster several children because she and her husband, who is Black, recognized that children needed and deserved a loving home, no matter their race. However, Jane always got the impression from the Home that it was inappropriate for her to take Black children in. She felt she was welcome to walk through the doors of the Home, sit at meetings, and help out, but "when it came to raising Black children," says Jane, "the sentiment was *this is where your welcome ends.*"

Jane recalls a particular situation when she tried to take four siblings in.

In the early 1980s I met a thirteen-year-old resident during a weekend event at the Home. She told me that she had two sisters and a brother. Over time, I watched her take on the mother role of her younger three siblings at the Home. Eventually I applied to take all of these children. We didn't believe in separating siblings. But even though we were willing to take in all of them, we were only allowed to take two. And their transition into our home was horrendous. The staff had no skills placing children and didn't seem to have any awareness of the emotional turmoil children experienced when transitioning to a new home.

Jane said the department, along with the social worker, also failed in its execution of the move. Starann, the little girl that Jane had met that weekend at the Home, would not be permitted

The Earle family provided a stable, loving home for Starann and her siblings.

to come with her two younger siblings. Jane recounted—and Starann later corroborated—that, in fact, no one ever told the girl that her younger brother and sister would be leaving.

Instead, they moved the kids while [Starann] was away in Toronto. No one told them why they were there, if they would ever return, or if they would ever see their two older siblings again. To compensate, I made sure when Starann returned, that the siblings received opportunities to spend time with each other. This was something I initiated on my own. There was no support or suggestion from staff or Community Services. It was also left up to us to make a way for the children to see their parents, with no facilitation or supervision by the department or the Home.

Jane and Starann say Starann resented this for many years; she felt that her siblings had been stolen from her. It wasn't until she reached adulthood that Starann described her anger to Jane and how she now has trouble trusting others.

When Jane became the Home's acting executive director, she had not been the original choice. The position was offered to her husband, Gordon Earle, while he was serving on the board. According to Jane, the former director had been let go due to incompetence. Ideally, Jane's husband would resign from the board and step into that role, the board had decided. However, the position was unpaid and only temporary until a permanent director could be hired. Jane had small children, including the couple's foster children, at home and the family couldn't afford to forego income. So Jane offered to take the unpaid job. The board called a meeting to decide if it would be a conflict of interest for Jane to take on the temporary role. Unanimously, the board agreed to allow her to step in and agreed to cover her child care costs at home.

Jane questioned whether the children were the priority, or if staff members' loyalties to each other came first. "That secrecy among staff was one of the first things I noticed," she says. "No one could prove something happened because staff would not speak about things they saw or heard. That was very frustrating."

In her 2012 affidavit to the courts as part of the class action launched by Wagners law firm, Child Welfare Consultant Sandra Scarth similarly noted, "[T]here seems to have been a conspiracy of silence.…[I]t appeared that protecting the reputation of staff members and the institution took precedence over the duty to protect the children in its care."

"One time there was a complaint that came to the board's attention," Jane says. "It was that some of the older boys had been committing sodomy on younger boys. We questioned the staff but no one would come forward to the board to address anything they may have seen." Jane's efforts to investigate the complaint proved futile. It wasn't until years later, when she was no longer working in that capacity at the Home, that she discovered those boys were mimicking what was being done to them by the Home's adult male staff. As many former residents began to confide in her as adults, Jane discovered that in many cases, male staff members were instigating the sexual acts the older boys were performing on the younger ones. Many former residents laid out similar, painful stories in affidavits supporting Wagners' class action suit, and alleged other staff knew what was going on, and never stopped it.

A culture of oppression and systemic discrimination was also at play. Jane discovered in her role as executive director that the Home was one of the most underfunded youth institutions in the province. When she came on board, the Home was nearly bankrupt. As discussed in Chapter 2, Jane felt that the per diems, supplied by the Province—raised to $27.88 in 1980—were appalling. The department, aware of the discrepancies at that time, did nothing. Its attitude towards minorities was a direct reflection of society's attitude towards Blacks and specifically Black children at that time. The department did not invest the money or resources into the children at the Home as they did for children in mainstream orphanages. The message internalized by the children who lived at the Home was, *we will not invest society's money and resources in to you or your future because you are not worth it.*

The Home, with its massive acreage, farming resources, and livestock, still had children who were malnourished. During her time as executive director, Jane began to question what happened to all the produce. Children were made to work out in the fields, weeding and harvesting. The idea was to teach them farming skills. But according to their testimonies, not all of them had the privilege of enjoying the harvest. June Elwin's affadavit states, "The boys were also shipped out to farms around Preston, Nova Scotia, to work on other farms as well. These farms belonged to friends of the staff. The boys received nothing for this labour." Although there is no direct evidence, rumours in the community claimed that staff members had taken some food for their own families. There was also talk that it was sold, but there is no accounting of the money.

When former residents began to come forward with accounts of abuse dating back to the 1940s, many there when Jane served as executive director reached out to her. Realizing there were many former residents carrying pain, Jane helped to form and provided counselling support through the Victims of Institutional Child Exploitation Society (VOICES). Established in 2012 by Jane and former residents Tony Smith and Tracey Dorrington, both of whom have been at the forefront of media coverage about the Home, VOICES is a non-profit advocasy organization that provides support to victims of institutional child exploitation and abuse. Jane was overcome with grief as she listened to former residents release the anguish they had carried for so many years. She began to think about what she had missed during her ten months as executive director. "I wonder if there were things I could have done better," she says. "Staff didn't come to me and tell me anything was wrong. I thought I had a good rapport with the children. I thought they would have come to me if something was wrong." Jane couldn't help but feel deep sorrow when several of them admitted, as adults, to being too afraid to come to her back then. In hindsight, Jane recalls several instances that were cause for concern, but admits it was almost impossible to investigate any issue when it came to questioning the staff.

Jane recalls an unforgettable encounter with a former resident: "I remember having seen a former staff member years ago
at a function where Rosa Parks was speaking. During our conversation, [the staff member] told me that she saw [the former
resident] in Truro and had learned some pretty awful stuff about
what happened to her when she was a child at the Home. That
resident told the staff member that she couldn't keep the dark
secrets in longer." That conversation would not leave Jane's mind.
She wanted to talk to that resident personally to see if she was
okay and to validate her experiences. Eventually Jane tracked the
resident down and asked to come and talk with her. The resident
agreed. What ensued was a three-hour conversation between
the two about the resident's horrific childhood experiences. "The
things she witnessed and the things that were done to her left me
devastated," Jane says.

*I kept apologizing to her for what she'd been through, even though
I wasn't directly responsible. I wanted to help her. I asked her
what she wanted to do about it. She said she didn't want to cause
trouble or embarrass her race [the staff members who caused her
pain were Black] but she desperately wanted the Home's Board of
Directors to hear her story and to know what happened to her and
the other children.*

Although she was no longer affiliated with the Home, Jane
wanted badly to help. She contacted the Home's executive director
and relayed the gut-wrenching story that the former resident had
told. "I thought for sure that the current board would definitely
want to hear this young woman's story and would want to work
towards some kind of resolution," Jane says. "So they initially set

up a meeting with just me, the chair of the board, and the director to discuss my concern. I also brought my husband [Gordon Earle] to that meeting with me as an advocate."

Her husband was a former MP for the New Democratic Party, Nova Scotia's first Black Member of Parliament, and a four-time New Democratic candidate. (He left the provincial NDP in 2013 because he felt the Dexter government was not appropriately handling the concerns about and allegations of abuse at the Home.) With her husband by her side, Jane entered into the meeting with hope. But shockingly, the director and chair vehemently stressed that they would not be meeting with the former resident: they did not want to hear any stories, and that if the resident felt she had been wronged she should just go to the police, Jane recounts. This response was shattering to the former resident who had already been so emotionally damaged and had already spent most of her life being "unheard."

Still, with remarkable tenacity, and Jane's help, the former resident found the courage to continue to tell her story in the hopes that other children would not go through what she did. It was the same for many other residents who contacted Jane and asked to talk; she provided support, a much needed visit, or simply listened. Jane became an ally and advocate.

Jane's history with child welfare in Canada goes back many years. Today, she remains a staunch advocate for survivors of childhood abuse. She consoles and counsels former residents of the Nova Scotia Home for Colored Children and continues to hear from others who have found the courage to come forward with their stories. Many former residents loudly sing her praises and have reported how fortunate they are to have had Jane in their corner fighting for them, helping them move toward healing.

When she first began serving as executive director at the Home, Jane acknowledges that she tried to correct some wrongs; she knew many of the staff members were not properly trained in child welfare. Reports paint a picture of pleas for increased funding that repeatedly fell on deaf ears. Jane says that when she became aware that physical punishment was used to discipline the children, she immediately raised her concerns to staff and ordered it to stop.

Looking back, it is probably more likely that staff continued to keep the incidents hidden. At the time when she handed down the directive, she states, Jane had no idea about the sexual abuse. However, she did recall that during a staff meeting, one of the male staff members asked if they he and his male colleagues would still be permitted in the girls' rooms. "I remember getting a creepy feeling about him back then," she says, "and now I know why he asked that question." That same staff member emerged as one of the key perpetrators former residents accuse of rape, beatings, and sending some former residents into a life of prostitution.

Jane is now a voice for those children who were wronged and firmly believes it is a social worker's ethical, moral, and legal responsibility to know what is going on with the children in their care.

Lillian Romkey

On September 13, 1948, social worker Lillian Romkey completed a three-paged report detailing her concerns following a visit to the Home. Among other things, she noted a huge discrepancy between what the staff fed the children and what they ate themselves. She recounted a time, during her visit, the children were about to sit down to a meal of fish chowder. After learning she was going to stay, the cook suddenly ordered that bread be cut and buttered. Romkey believed that had she not decided to stay and observe, the children would not have received the bread: "I feel sure that the children would have received no other item for lunch except the Fish Chowder if we had not come on the scene," read the report. In describing the chowder, Romkey noted it was a mixture of fish bones, potatoes, and milk. One of the children complained out loud that there was no fish in his bowl, said Romkey. No fish could be found anywhere. The children received nothing else to eat. However, the staff meal, according to Romkey, consisted of fried halibut, vegetable soup, carrots, sliced tomatoes, pickles, potatoes, and fresh apple pie.

A month later, in October 1948, Ms. Romkey paid another visit to the Home at mealtime. Again, as the meal was being prepared, the social worker indicated that she heard staff in the kitchen scramble to put out bread for the children after she announced she was staying. In her notes, Romkey said she was convinced bread and milk were not a regular part of the children's meal. On that day, the children were served what Romkey called a "concoction" of potatoes and turnips cut into big squares that sat in boiling water. The water made it appear like a soup. Some of the bread was covered with a thin spread of jam or butter. She said that she and the worker who accompanied her examined the meal carefully and determined that there was no meat included, just the potatoes, turnips, and water. The staff had roast chicken that day, said Romkey. In her recommendations to Mr. MacKinnon, Ms. Romkey said she believed the children were not receiving adequate food and urged the members of the board be approached regarding the children's meals. There is no record to suggest that either Mr. MacKinnon or his department ever followed up on Ms. Romkey's recommendations.

Anne Keith

Anne Keith served as supervisor for the Department of Community Services and worked in the field of social work for over fifty years. Anne recalls throughout that time, during the early 1970s and '80s, that provincial social workers were "flying by the seat of their pants." In Nova Scotia, social work up until that time provided very few guidelines and no concrete standards of practice or accountability. "The organization of the social work profession in Canada did not begin until the early part of the twentieth century," states a 2010 report completed by social workers Bessie Harris and Harold Beals for the Nova Scotia Association of Social Workers. Social work was about practicality and getting the job done. It wasn't until several decades later that the focus on casework and standards became more of a priority. The report suggests that it wasn't until the mid-1950s, when the subject of licensure arose, that there was growing interest in recognizing social work as a profession. "At this point in time," reads the report, "social work had still not gained sufficient stature as a profession to garner the support needed to bring about licensure." Social work practice still had a long way to go in terms of professional ethics and accountability.

During her tenure, Anne was a champion on the front lines in the creation and implementation of standards for social workers. Working out of the Community Services professional building in Dartmouth, Windsor, and other areas, she recognized the need to improve the practice of social work. She implemented planning goals for the workers under her charge. She insisted that all children be accounted for. As she discussed caseloads with her team, she expected updates on each child and the worker's involvement.

Anne describes social work practice back then as being mostly directed by the priorities of the supervisor. Some were excellent but others were not. For the most part, workers did as they were told and simply abided by whatever direction came down from the top, good or bad. Anne also recalls there were many restrictions and control by higher-ups: bosses and district supervisors. Sometimes power and control overshadowed or hindered the process of good social work practice and accountability. With Anne's strong desire to improve standards, she questioned the motivation behind the relocation of the province's School for Boys to the Shelburne area. She was among many who felt that the children there were too far removed from much needed resources.

In 1948 the Department of Welfare took over what was formerly The Halifax Industrial School for Boys after it was scheduled for closure due to lack of funds. After renaming it the Nova Scotia Facility for Boys only a year later, the department relocated the facility to rural Shelburne. "People questioned the motivation for it, and whether it was a good idea to locate the school so far away from services provided in urban centres like Halifax and Yarmouth, " read the 2002 Kaufman Report—an in-depth inquiry and independent review of Nova Scotia's response to institutional abuse headed up by former Quebec judge Fred Kaufman—"The move to Shelburne also made it more difficult for most families to visit their children."

Soon after the move, the facility allegedly became a breeding ground for sexual predators. The allegations of former residents date back nearly to the founding of the institution. As adults, many of the boys would come forward to share stories of alleged sexual abuse at the hands of male staff.

Anne was the supervisor of one such worker who was eventually charged with abuses against children. Cesar Lalo was employed by the Department of Community Services from 1971 to 1989. He began as a caseworker and was responsible for several wards in the department. "During that time, I was his supervisor," says Anne, "but I had no idea he was a predator." He later moved on the Shelburne School for Boys. In 2004 he was found guilty of sexually assaulting twenty-nine boys from 1973 to 1989 during his time as a social worker and probation officer for the Province of Nova Scotia, and was sentenced to eleven years in prison.

The Kaufman Report suggested that at the Shelburne School for Boys, policies were implemented not in relation to sexual abuse, but to the physical abuse of boys. The policy restricted the use of punishment by force. Staff was not permitted to strike any of the residents with anything besides the permitted strap—which, although unacceptable by today's standards, was common practice in 1948, when these policies were drafted. And still, the existence of such policies indicates that officials were aware of incidences of abuse in youth institutions. There are no records to indicate that those same provincial officials expressed concern about physical abuse at the Nova Scotia Home for Colored Children, even though documents do suggest they were aware of such incidents.

In the history of the Association of Social Workers document, Mr. MacKinnon was heralded as "an intelligent man, a well-respected bureaucrat, a great orator and a man with a vision of social welfare for the future." Seen as a trailblazer in the field of social work, having served in key roles such as Director of Child welfare and Deputy Minister of Social Services, Mr. MacKinnon was instrumental in championing many of the gains made in the field. In 1959 in his report to the minister, Mr. MacKinnon, as director of Child Welfare, stated that although corporal punishment had been used at the Nova Scotia Facility for Boys in the past, it was no longer appropriate, no longer to be used. MacKinnon said that beatings and punishment were not as effective in caring for children as understanding and discipline.

The directive may have demonstrated great insight and compassion on Mr. MacKinnon's part—but appeared to extend only to mainstream institutions. Had Mr. MacKinnon displayed that same amount of concern and direction for the Home and the residents who were suffering daily, hundreds of children would have been spared habitually cruel beatings that left them begging for mercy. It wasn't until the 1990s that Mr. MacKinnon's officials developed policies surrounding sexual abuse at the Shelburne School for Boys. The Home, which closed in 1989, never saw any such policies put in place.

Anne recalls there were "assumed" child protection policies in the very early part of her career predating the Children and Family Services Act, which lays out legislation aimed at protecting children. Directives were not written in stone, she says. According to a Nova Scotia Association of Social Work document on social work pioneers, "Children's Aid Societies need an injection of professionally educated social workers but there were no such individuals available in Nova Scotia, and people who were sent to other provinces to receive the much needed education rarely returned to Nova Scotia." Anne says that social workers in

Nova Scotia were expected to keep track of the children in their care and make follow-up visits to the foster homes and institutions where their wards were placed. As discovered many years later in reports, many social workers in the field fabricated reports or didn't complete any at all. Because there were no written rules, social workers made decisions as they went along.

Anne left the field in the 1980s, but she hopes her efforts and commitment to enforcing better standards and accountability in the profession have contributed in some way to the betterment of children in care. Anne was on the Public Relations Committee when the Association of Social Workers published its first newsletter in 1966, for which she, along with the committee, served as editor. The newsletter would serve as a vehicle to further the goals and objectives of the association and share its work and accomplishments in the profession. In 1985, while serving as chair of the Public Relations Committee, Anne reported to the council that the newsletter was reorganizing its focus to concentrate more on fostering awareness of issues in the profession and would be professionally published. By December 1986, the newsletter was labelled with its new name, *Connections*, and scheduled for publication three times a year. Today, *Connections* serves as an invaluable resource for the profession, and has expanded to further include important book reviews and innovative techniques for social work practice. Anne credits Rosemary Rippon for blazing a trail in the fight to improve standards and develop policies to address the needs and best interests of children in care.

Rosemary Rippon

Rosemary Rippon was a social worker with the Department of Community Services and a long-time member of the Nova Scotia Association of Social Workers (NSASW). Her files from those years of social work proved to be an invaluable resource and now remain a part of the NSASW archives. After moving from England to Canada with her parents in 1951, Rosemary joined the staff of the Lunenburg County Children's Aid Society and became its executive director in 1958. Rosemary accepted a role as coordinator for Foster Home Services in 1966 and was subsequently promoted to director of Children and Family Services, under which title she served until her retirement in 1991.

In 1966, while coordinator for Foster Home Services, Rosemary visited the Nova Scotia Home for Colored Children to prepare a report on its functioning. When she arrived the Home had seventy-five residents, its highest number ever. She concluded that the Home was terribly overcrowded and that the children were not receiving proper medical assessments upon arrival. One child had been admitted with a highly contagious disease.

"From talking with the Superintendent it would appear that the children placed in the institution are there not primarily to meet their needs, but rather to meet the needs of agencies who are lacking in foster homes," read Rippon's report. She also noted an insufficient number of staff: there were only sixteen employees, none of whom had any child care training. She noted that the workers in the Home received very low wages, well below the provincial minimum. "There is no personal policy outlining job description, minimum qualifications, hours of work, etc. To engage and hold good staff nowadays, good working conditions together with dedication are a must," the report continued.

These issues, coupled with a lack of funds to provide training, and repeated denials by the director of Child Welfare, Dr. Fred MacKinnon, of requests for increased funding contributed to Rosemary Rippon's less-than-favourable review. There is no evidence to suggest the Province made changes or increased funds as a result of her report.

———

For the purposes of obtaining input from all sides, two social workers responsible for placing wards in the Home were contacted to provide their perspectives in this book. Many former residents wanted an explanation as to why so many social workers failed to maintain contact after placing them there. Both declined.

———

These pioneering women fought on the front lines to change policies, and as a result gains have been made in the practice of social work. There is still more work to be done in terms of equality and fairness in government and within organizations; however, greater awareness within the social work profession, increased accountability in child welfare practice, mandatory training and professional development for social workers, and oversight from governing bodies such as the social work associations across Canada have helped to lessen both the prevalence and degree of unjust and unethical practices.

Chapter 12

The Apology:
Where Do We Go *from* Here?

AFTER OVER A DECADE OF struggle, the approval notice of the settlement agreement between former residents of the Nova Scotia Home for Colored Children and the Province of Nova Scotia was laid out for all to see: the July 7, 2014, issue of the Halifax *Chronicle-Herald* let the province know the journey had finally come to a diplomatic conclusion. The apology further affirmed and acknowledged that children who lived at the Home between 1921 and 1989 had experienced trauma, and directly or indirectly suffered as a result. The Province agreed to pay $29 million to former residents. This settlement was combined with the $5 million settlement from the Home in July 2013.

The first part of that settlement falls under what was called the Common Experience Payment, described in court papers as "an acknowledgment of aspects of your experience and a symbolic compensation for former residents, for the harmful aspects of your shared experiences at the Home." That meant all residents shared a common experience at the Home, causing them harm. Common Experience Payment amounts were determined by the length of time a former resident lived at the Home. Those who lived there under forty days received $1,000. Those who lived there between forty days and one year received $10,000. Those who resided there for over a year were eligible to receive the $10,000 plus an additional $3,000 for each subsequent year.

The second part of the settlement is called the Independent Assessment Process Payment. This was set aside for former residents who experienced severe harm outside of the common experience, including incidences of rape, severe corporal punishment, injuries, and so on. Payment under this stream required the individual to recount their experiences to independent experts who would determine whether it was outside of the "common experience," and if so, decide the level of harm. A claims evaluator would then assess payment. In general, there were four levels of compensation under this stream. Level one: significant harm, $25,000. Level two: very significant harm, $50,000. Level three: severe harm, $100,000. Level four: very severe harm, $200,000. Under this stream, former residents could also claim counselling costs. Although money could never erase the damage that was done, it was a big step forward in an attempt to compensate former residents for the disadvantages they have experienced as a result of living at the Home.

The next step came three months later: one year after Premier Stephen McNeil was elected, he followed through on an election promise. On October 10, 2014, political leaders, the media, and former residents of the Nova Scotia Home for Colored Children gathered in the provincial legislature building to hear the premier issue a public apology on behalf of the Province for the abuses suffered by former residents for over fifty years. For former residents this was long-overdue confirmation that the government finally acknowledged their suffering. Former residents like Stephanie Langford feel that, although she still awaits justice for her deceased brother, the apology was an important step towards healing. It appears below.

"Apology to Former Residents of the Nova Scotia Home for Colored Children"

On behalf of the Government of Nova Scotia, I apologize to those who suffered abuse and neglect at the Nova Scotia Home for Colored Children.

It is one of the great tragedies in our province's history that your cries for help were greeted with silence for so long.

Some of you have said you felt invisible. You are invisible no longer. We hear your voices and we grieve for your pain. We are sorry.

Some of you faced horrific abuse that no child should ever experience. You deserved a better standard of care. For the trauma and neglect you endured, and their lingering effects on you and your loved ones, we are truly sorry.

We thank you for showing such courage and perseverance in telling your stories. Your strength, your resilience, and your desire for healing and reconciliation should be an inspiration to all Nova Scotians.

To the African Nova Scotian community: we are sorry. The struggle of the Home is only one chapter in a history of systemic racism and inequality that has scarred our province for generations.

African Nova Scotians are a founding culture in our province—a resourceful people of strength. The Home for Colored Children was birthed in the community as a way to meet a need that was not being met.

We must acknowledge that in many ways, and for many years, we as a province have not adequately met the needs of African Nova Scotian children and their families. We are sorry.

As Nova Scotians—as a people, walking together—we must do better.

An apology is not a closing of the books, but a recognition that we must cast an unflinching eye on the past as we strive toward a better future.

We are sorry for your suffering, we are grateful for your courage, and we welcome your help in building a healthier future for all of us.

After other parties in power had ignored the pleas, the letters, and the cries for help over the last decade, the newly elected Liberal government made it a priority to recognize the injustices suffered by the former residents of the Nova Scotia Home for Colored Children and the resulting hardships. The admission that these injustices were so deeply rooted in systemic racist and discriminatory practices was a vital acknowledgement for the community. It was the confirmation that stifled all those who accused social advocates of "playing the race card." The very system put in place for the protection of its people was flawed and defective. Now that Nova Scotia's provincial government had finally opened the door, it was up to the community to step through it and help facilitate the changes needed to ensure a tragedy of this magnitude doesn't happen again.

The formal apology and final class-action settlement were steps in the right direction. It had been a very long road to that point, close to seventeen years for some, like June Elwin. Older former residents would never see their abusers, since passed away, brought to justice. "The woman who abused me is gone," Garnet says. He knows he will never hear her say she is sorry. Abusers who are still alive have never been and most likely will never be charged with a crime or serve time in jail. RCMP have indicated that the lack of evidence, police reports, medical records, and the amount of time that has passed prevents them from proceeding with any further action against the accused. So as former residents come to terms with those facts, the healing must move forward.

In his speech to a crowd gathered at Emmanuel Baptist Church in Hammonds Plains, Nova Scotia, on June 8, 2015, Premier McNeil stood before a crowd of elected officials, former residents, and concerned citizens to release details about its upcoming restorative inquiry. Expected to begin in December 2015, it is slated to take two years. During the process, former residents will have an opportunity to share their experiences in a safe space, in the form of group sessions. The inquiry also allows former residents to say out loud what happened to them and explain how the system failed them.

The inquiry's goal is to understand what really happened at the Nova Scotia Home for Colored Children. It is also a means for everyone involved to move forward. It will be overseen by government representatives, members of the Black community, the Home's representatives, and most importantly, former residents.

In November 2015, the Nova Scotia government appointed a twelve-member Council of Parties to oversee the inquiry. The panel includes Mike Dull, non-voting legal advisor and lawyer for the successful class action suit; Jean Flynn, premier's representative; Wayn Hamilton, provincial government representative; Shawna Hoyte and Joan Jones, community representatives; Jennifer Llewellyn, restorative process advisor (non-voting); Gerry Morrison and Tony Smith, VOICES representatives; LaMeia Reddick, community youth representative; Sylvia Parris, Nova Scotia Home for Colored Children Board representative; Chief Judge Pamela Williams, judicial representative, and Carolann Wright-Parks, restorative inquiry coordinating director. An official opening is slated to take place prior to the commencement of the inquiry. The Council of Parties will provide guidance and oversee the $5 million inquiry, while a task force hopes to emerge with a review of what has been learned and provide recommendations.

A main goal of the inquiry is to make sure it remains a forum for healing, not for blame. The hope is that former residents, including those who have been reluctant to speak in the past, will take advantage of the opportunity to finally be heard, share their experiences, and move forward. As they continue to share their stories, the load will get lighter. For society, the hope is that the inquiry will serve as a positive step forward, and that those former residents who have experienced trauma as a result of living in the Home will receive comfort and the courage to continue on a path towards restoration and healing. For the Black Nova Scotian community, the hope is that the Home can right its wrongs. Being a voice at the table during the inquiry, as it intends to be, is an important step towards that goal.

"We know that one inquiry will not solve every issue of racism and equality in Nova Scotia," McNeil stated, "but we're hopeful this will mark a new beginning and a new way forward, one that we can walk together. Some painful truths will come to light over the life of this inquiry. The results will challenge us to do things differently."

The Road Toward Healing

A Shared Responsibility

IT IS NOW THE DUTY of all Canadian provinces to mandate that professionals working with children and the general public report suspected abuse to the authorities—either to police or child welfare agencies (Trocmé et al., 2010). Children now have the right to be protected from violence and maltreatment through both national and international laws and conventions. The United Nations, of which Canada is a ratifying member, recognizes through the Convention on the Rights of the Child (1989) that all children are entitled to human rights. That includes the right to be protected from violence and harm and to be properly cared for. More locally, each province and territory has child protection legislation under the Criminal Code to ensure those rights are upheld. In Nova Scotia for instance, the Children and Family Services Act includes laws to provide for intervention when a child is in need of protection.

While these laws exist and are upheld, the issue often has to do with education. Sometimes when an abusive act is perpetrated upon a child, the adult responsible is not aware that his or her actions are indeed abusive. Internal factors such as limited knowledge of child development and external factors such as lack of education can contribute to the incidence and degrees of abuse. "Child maltreatment" is a term used to describe abusive acts perpetrated by adults or older youth against young children and can fall into any of the following four categories: physical abuse, sexual abuse, emotional abuse, and neglect.

Physical abuse can consist of a slap, kick, punch, hit, or any other physically violent contact with the body. Injuries sustained can range from minor to severe and can even result in permanent bodily injury or death. While physical punishment is largely a thing of the past, parents who still use it as a means of discipline need to be aware that the Children and Family Services Act indicates that punishment such as beating with an object, weapon, or closed fist crosses the line, can be grounds for an investigation into abuse, and can seriously injure or kill a child.

Sexual abuse involves inappropriate acts of a sexual nature that directly or indirectly involve an underage child. This includes wanted or unwanted fondling, sexual solicitation, harassment, exposure to or of genitals/private areas, intercourse, and other sexual acts. An underage child cannot, by law, consent to sex. Therefore the perpetrator is committing an illegal act when engaging in any form of sexual contact with a child. Currently, Canadian law states that the age of consent is sixteen years, which was raised from fourteen years in 2008. Exceptions arise, for instance, in cases where both parties are underaged and/or the perpetrator is less than two years older than the victim.

Emotional abuse of a child is the damage that you can't physically see. Manipulation, degradation, humiliation, and verbally abusive acts such as name-calling and uttering threats can all leave emotional scars that can make a child feel worthless and can cause low self-esteem. While the scars of emotional abuse may be unseen, they may never heal.

Child neglect refers to a parent or caregiver's failure to provide a child with the necessities of life, such as food, clothing, shelter, love, and medical attention. Often, a child living in poverty is mistaken for a neglected child. Just because a person is poor, it doesn't mean they do not love and care for their child. Before stricter oversight began to take place in the last few decades, social workers and children's aid societies removed children from their homes simply because the parents were considered poor and didn't possess adequate resources. Child protection workers must be careful not to skew the lines between a parent who is neglectful and one who is in need of support to help provide the necessities of life to their children.

Seriously neglected children are at a higher risk of developing long-term problems. Despite that, treatment for abused and neglected children has been historically disjointed. This is due in part to too few treatment programs and too little emphasis on the acute emotional needs of these children. Many eventually move into adulthood with a deficiency, not having received the proper treatment necessary to become healthy and well-functioning members of society. While some thrive despite the odds, others may develop alternate ways of coping, such as withdrawal or substance abuse. Others may fall into depression, experience failure in their relationships, or continue on with self-destructive behaviours.

Increased education and awareness are needed to help service providers such as teachers, school counsellors, and coaches identify children in crisis. A greater understanding of how the child welfare system works will go a long way to improving the way child protection concerns are handled and how efficiently the system can work to provide for the needs and best interests of children. The duty to report suspected abuse is one of the most commonly misunderstood tenets of the child welfare system. According to Canada's Child Welfare Act, *everybody* has a duty to report any suspected abuse of a child. The law does not require a person to know for certain that abuse has occurred; their duty is to report what they suspect. It is then up to trained, front-line child welfare social workers to investigate further and determine whether abuse has occurred.

The misunderstanding occurs when people express reluctance to report because they feel it's just a hunch or they don't have enough evidence. In my thirteen years of experience as a social worker and case manager in Nova Scotia and Ontario—and prior to that, as an early childhood educator—teachers and doctors, high on the list of those with the closest contact with children, were sometimes the most reluctant to report any suspected abuse. There could be many reasons for this, for instance not wanting to testify in court or a familiarity with the family that leads to hesitancy. I experienced many incidents as a child protection worker where a school principal made the call to child welfare to report on behalf of a reluctant teacher who suspects a student is being abused; however, if the principal is relaying second-hand information, the teacher will still need to be interviewed to obtain the first-hand information necessary to fully investigate the case. It is important that those in a position to have eyes on society's children on a consistent basis work through their fear of reporting and become an ally for the child. Many more victims—those who may never come forward themselves or may not have an adult they trust—could be spared needless and senseless abuse.

In my personal experience, I've found it necessary to evaluate how my childhood story affected my adult life and how the circumstances surrounding my journey have led me on this path. I think about my brother, who never received the help he needed from the Home or from the social worker assigned to his case. How the absolute trauma of being a child and watching a car hit his mother, laying afterward in a pool of blood, may have affected him later in life. I've had to examine how difficult it was for my sister, who only recently wrote down her feelings for the first time, to come to terms with how she was affected by living in the Home. I never really understood her trauma until I heard her read it out loud. I've had to think about how the past still haunts another brother, a victim of violent abuse at the Home, who still refuses to even mention the place.

I have witnessed the very different ways of coping exhibited by others I know who lived at the Home. Some still carry their grief and pain, so much so that it has cast a dark shadow over their adult lives. Even when I tell people that I was in foster care, I know the first thought is that I was neglected or abused. I feel compelled to explain; I often don't. But I can relate to some of the Home's former residents when they tell me they are ashamed to tell people they lived there. The feeling we share is that people automatically think we must be *damaged goods*. So not only do former residents have to conquer the hurdles of their own pain and trauma; they also have to navigate a society that prejudges them based on their past and how much they can accomplish in their future.

Former residents of the Home cannot change or ignore what happened to them. They own the cards they were dealt. The question is, how do they play out the rest of their lives? Finding and embracing their realities is a part of the healing. There is no right or wrong way to heal and no timeframe for making that happen. For some, it may take years, and for others, it may take the rest of their lives. Each of the Home's abuse survivors experienced and internalized their trauma in different ways. And as each person's experience differs, so too does their healing. Take Richard, who experienced difficulty in his earlier relationships because of his past; or Lisa, who has kept herself fairly isolated as a form of protection and has always felt unwanted.

In 1999 the Morris Center in San Francisco, California, published a manual called *Survivor to Thriver* for adult survivors of childhood abuse. In it, the authors outline various stages of healing that remain relevant today. A few of its insights are included in this chapter along with research from others in the field, such as the Advocacy Center, as well as suggestions that former residents claim have helped them. The following guide I developed is not all encompassing and may not work for every survivor, but the hope is that it will normalize the experiences of abuse survivors and provide them with hope for their journey ahead. It is not meant to be a directive but simply may be helpful for those who wish to use it to find healing, or at least, I hope, some contentment in knowing they are not alone.

Make the decision to try and heal: This is a choice you must make as an individual, one that takes incredible strength, insight, and commitment. Some people go through a stage of denial, during which they are not ready to deal with the pain. In other cases, the trauma is so severe that it has been shut out as a form of coping. But once you have come to a realization that something happened, you must choose what you will do with that experience. The road will not be easy, but making a choice to try and heal is an important first step.

Expect continued feelings of panic and crisis: Many former residents feel consumed by thoughts of the abuse they suffered, as if it happened yesterday. For them, life can often feel like a constant state of emergency, where nothing is going right and bad things seem to keep happening. Some describe it as feeling stuck. Know that sometimes panicky feelings will emerge when you begin to make connections between your past and how it affects your present. These feelings are normal.

Risk telling others: Former residents who have spoken out about their abuse have risked having others view them differently or refuse to believe their stories. Many have noted they have had to relive their trauma each time they spoke about it. Despite this possibility, breaking the silence is a very powerful step towards healing. Sometimes sharing experiences with others can also be a source of strength. Reaching out, getting counselling, and sharing with others who have experienced similar trauma will help you cope with the stress. These are important steps in healing and will help shift your focus from those damaging thoughts to a more positive perspective.

Understand that you *can* heal: Once you are able to open up and talk about the experience, a sense of relief may follow. Understanding your trauma can sometimes help you to understand the pain associated with it.

Take blame away from yourself: Sometimes survivors of childhood abuse blame themselves for what happened. But any abuse perpetrated upon a child is *never* the child's fault. In the Home, in some cases, older residents who were also being victimized were made by staff members to commit abusive acts on others. Even in these cases, the blame belongs to the adult perpetrators, the system, and the professionals responsible for the safety and well-being of the children in their care.

Embrace the grieving process: This means allowing yourself to feel the way you feel about the situation, without excusing or ignoring it. It's okay to be sad. Many who have experienced physical and sexual abuse or neglect at the Home will grieve in a variety of ways. Some will grieve for their lost childhoods, for the child within them that was so broken and damaged. Others will grieve over how they were hurt or mistreated by others throughout their lives or because they weren't protected. Regardless, the process of grieving is real and is necessary to help purge those painful feelings. Embracing it doesn't mean you're saying what happened is okay. It means you are agreeing that *how* you feel about what happened is okay.

Expect anger and depression: It is perfectly normal for former residents to express feelings of anger and frustration. The source of their anger stems from a range of places: anger that the government didn't protect them; anger that the adults in their lives got away with mistreating them for so long; anger that when they finally did find the courage to tell, no one listened; anger that when they went public with their stories, society refused to believe anything happened and questioned their motives. They are also angry that those responsible for the abuse have never admitted to their crimes and will never be brought to justice. Some even express anger over what happened in their families that brought them into care in the first place. However, it is important that survivors use their anger as energy to fuel positive change and not to create more inward turmoil. Thoughts of sadness and mild depression are common but should they turn into feelings of hopelessness, you should seek the help of a professional.

Forgive: Some abuse survivors are able to get to a point where they decide to forgive in order to move on, but may never forget. For others, forgiveness may not be part of the healing process. Forgiving a person who wronged you is a way to reclaim authority and control over your life, but if you are unable, it doesn't mean that you won't continue to heal. Forgiveness carries a lot of weight. Before you even begin to decide whether or not you will forgive the person or people who hurt you, the first person who needs forgiveness is you. Sometimes victims feel guilt over their experiences, or feel they could have done more to prevent what they saw or what happened to them. Sometimes victims become victimizers themselves, as was the case with those children in the Home who began abusing other residents. The guilt associated with actions that you can never take back is tremendous. It can become too much for one person to bear. But by removing blame and forgiving yourself, you are slowly reclaiming power.

Tap into your spiritual self: A strong spiritual grounding is an excellent source of strength, power, inspiration, love, and all of the elements a survivor needs to self-heal. Some former residents claim to have tapped deep into their spirituality as they move through their healing process and through that, they say they gain greater strength and understanding.

Move on: Eventually, most former residents will get to the point where they feel life has become manageable, when they are not constantly in a state of emotional turmoil. Some may already be there and others may never get there, but healing is a very long process. There will be high and low times. Some days you will feel like the world is okay and other days you may feel wronged. But as you work through it, you will feel less in crisis and more in control of life.

There will always be individuals who are angry about what happened at the Home, just as there will always be those who deny anything ever took place.

With increased accountability, institutions that house troubled, abandoned, and parentless youth are expected to provide an environment where children are nurtured, feel wanted, and are able to thrive. As a former foster child, I support policies and regulations (such as the Children and Family Services Act, the Social Work Act, and the Disabilities Act) that serve as efficient methods to keep agencies accountable. In my own family's case, the lack of regulations and oversight led to systemic flaws. Children in care have a right to know how they got there. Case records must be created and preserved so that foster children and others in care can return and put together the pieces of their past. It is not acceptable to simply be told by government officials, "We have no idea—no record—of what happened to you when we were your 'parent.'" While I know that I will never find my answers, I am encouraged that future foster children will.

For the former residents of the Home who have faced insurmountable odds, overcome great obstacles, and continue to push their way through the pain of their childhoods, I commend you for your tenacity and courage. For those who have yet to come to terms with their past, I hope that after having read the stories of others, you will realize you are not to blame; you are not alone. Healing may begin at the individual level, but it also includes government, representatives of the Home, and society. These entities, too, are making strides in the healing process.

As a social worker, part of my contribution to the healing is writing this book: to examine the societal and institutional structures at play that led to this tragedy and to provide a platform in which former residents may share their stories. My work is not complete.

We as a society are still inadequately protecting children from harm. We have the capacity, intelligence, and expertise to develop and design enhanced policies to protect our vulnerable citizens. We say that children are our future, but at a government level, they are often the last to be discussed and the first to be exploited by policies that don't meet their needs.

Everyone has a part to play to support former residents of the Nova Scotia Home for Colored Children, other children in care now, and those who will be in the future. For generations to come, the stories of the Home's former residents will be shared. It is also my hope that those involved—former residents, families that have been broken, severed, or otherwise affected—can come together to heal from their pain. These stories should become lessons. We leave this chapter, not forgetting the past but moving forward, and acknowledging this: the *hurt* was real, the *hope* is certain, and the *healing* will soon triumph.

Selected Bibliography

Bagley, Chris. "Child Sexual Abuse and Juvenile Prostitution: A Commentary on the Badgley Report on Sexual Offences Against Children and Youth." *Canadian Journal of Public Health*, Vol. 76, January/February 1985, 65–66.

Binggeli, Nelson J., Stuart N. Hart, and Marla R. Brassard. *Psychological Maltreatment of Children*. Thousand Oaks, California: Sage Publications, 2001.

Brooke, James. "Shelburne Journal; Tales of Sex, Violence and Greed in a Small Town." *The New York Times* online. January 13, 2000.

Cahill, Barry. "Paths to the Law in Late-Victorian Africadia: The Odyssey of James Robinson Johnston." Nova Scotia Barristers' Society online, 2012.

———. "The 'Colored Barrister': the short life and tragic death of James Robinson Johnston, 1876–1915." *Dalhousie Law Journal* (Halifax), Vol. 15, 1992, 336–79.

Centre of Excellence for Child Welfare. Canadian Child Welfare Research Portal, 2009. cwrp.ca

Dalhousie University. "Professor David Divine." James R. Johnston Chair in Black Canadian Studies: History of the Chair. Halifax: Dalhousie online.

Divine, David. *Aberlour Narratives of Success*. Durham, UK: Durham University, School of Applied Social Sciences, 2013.

Ginzberg, Lori D. *Women and the Work of Benevolence: Morality, Politics, and Class in the Nineteenth-Century United States*. New Haven, CT: Yale University, 1990.

Harris, Bessie, and Harold Beals. *The Nova Scotia Association of Social Workers: Part I, A History, 1963–2010*. Nova Scotia Association of Social Workers online. nsasw.org/document/1695/Master2.pdf

Jennissen, Therese, and Colleen Lundy. *One Hundred Years of Social Work: A History of the Profession in English Canada, 1900–2000*. Waterloo, ON: Wilfrid Laurier University, 2011.

Johnston, Justin Marcus. *James Robinson Johnston: The Life, Death and Legacy of Nova Scotia's First Black Lawyer*. Halifax: Nimbus, 2005.

Jones, Andrew, and Leonard Rutman. *In the Children's Aid: J. J. Kelso and Child Welfare in Ontario*. Toronto: University of Toronto, 1981.

Kaufman, Fred. *Searching For Justice: An Independent Review of Nova Scotia's Response to Institutional Abuse.* Vol. 1, Ch. 2. Government of Nova Scotia, January 2002.

Lafferty, Renée N. *The Guardianship of Best Interests: Institutional Care for the Children of the Poor in Halifax, 1850–1960.* Montreal: McGill-Queen's, 2013.

Malarek, Victor. *The Throwaway Children.* CTV News online: W5. November 3, 2012.

The Morris Center. *Survivor to Thriver.* San Francisco: The Morris Centre, 1995.

O'Connor, Stephen. *Orphan Trains: The Story of Charles Loring Brace and the Children he Saved and Failed.* Chicago: University of Chicago, 2001.

Ogrodnik, Lucie. "Child and Youth Victims of Police-reported Violent Crime, 2008." Statistics Canada: Canadian Centre for Justice Statistics Profile Series. Catalogue no. 85F0033X. No. 23, 2010.

———. "Spousal violence and repeat police contact." L. Ogrodnik (ed.) *Family Violence in Canada: A Statistical Profile, 2006.* Statistics Canada Catalogue no. 85-224-X, 2006.

Premier's Office, Province of Nova Scotia. "Province Apologizes to Former Residents of Nova Scotia Home for Colored Children." Delivered by Premier Stephen McNeil, October 10, 2014.

Saunders, Charles R. *Share & Care: The Story of the Nova Scotia Home for Colored Children.* Halifax: Nimbus, 1994.

Sinclair, Raven. "Identity lost and found: Lessons from the sixties scoop." *First Peoples Child & Family Review.* Vol. 3, 1, pp. 65–82, 2007.

Trocmé, N. "Child maltreatment and its impact on psychosocial child development epidemiology." Tremblay R. E, Barr R. G., Peters R. DeV., eds. *Encyclopedia on Early Childhood Development* online. Montreal: Centre of Excellence for Early Childhood Development, 2005, 1-5.

Wagners–A Serious Injury Law Firm. "NSHCC Settlement." Wagners online.

The author also acknowledges the Halifax Chronicle-Herald *and Supreme Court of Canada archives.*